BALL AND HAMMER

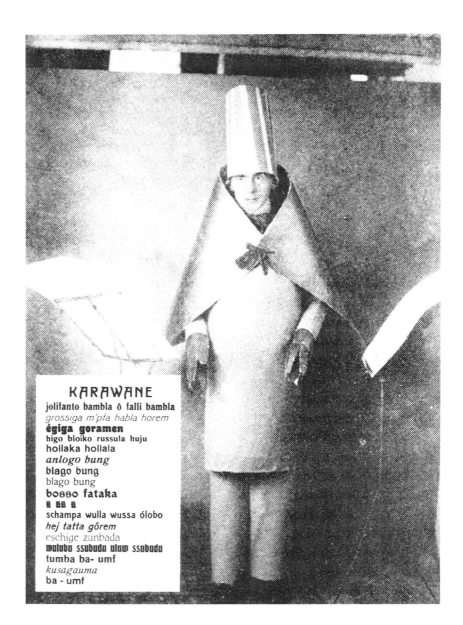

HUGO BALL, 1916.

BALL AND HAMMER

Hugo Ball's *TENDERENDA THE FANTAST*
Illustrated by JONATHAN HAMMER

Translated and with an essay by JONATHAN HAMMER

Introduced, edited, and annotated by JEFFREY T. SCHNAPP

YALE UNIVERSITY PRESS
NEW HAVEN AND LONDON

PUBLISHED WITH SUPPORT FROM MATTHEW MARKS GALLERY, NEW YORK.

DESIGNED BY MARY VALENCIA. SET IN TRUMP MEDIEVAL, UNIVERS, AND ROSEWOOD FILL TYPE BY INTEGRATED PUBLISHING SOLUTIONS, GRAND RAPIDS, MICHIGAN. PRINTED IN ITALY.

ISBN 0-300-08373-4 (CLOTH: ALK. PAPER) LIBRARY OF CONGRESS CONTROL NUMBER 2002105117

CATALOGUE RECORDS FOR THIS BOOK ARE AVAILABLE FROM THE BRITISH LIBRARY AND THE LIBRARY OF CONGRESS. THE PAPER IN THIS BOOK MEETS THE GUIDELINES FOR PERMANENCE AND DURABILITY OF THE COMMITTEE ON PRODUCTION GUIDELINES FOR BOOK LONGEVITY OF THE COUNCIL ON LIBRARY RESOURCES.

10 9 8 7 6 5 4 3 2 1

CONTENTS

ACKNOWLEDGMENTS

It has taken more than twenty years for this book to arrive at its final form. The bulk of the translation was begun at Bard College in 1979, with the invaluable help of Justus Rosenberg. I then put the manuscript aside until the 1990s, when I began the initial books and drawings that accompany the text, finished the translation, and wrote the essay. I wish to thank the many galleries, curators, and museums that have shown my related visual work. In Cologne, the Daniel Buchholz Gallery; in Berlin, the Neu Gallery; in London, the Lotta Hammer Gallery; in Madrid, the Fucares Gallery; in San Francisco, the jennjoygallery; and in Columbus, Ohio, the wonderful Rebecca Ibel Gallery.

I would especially like to thank the Swiss Arts Council (Pro Helvetia) most particularly Dr. Eggenberger and Ms. Cassuth, for allowing me the funds to further my work in Switzerland. For the many months I spent in Zurich I thank the Peter Kilchmann Gallery. Peter was an important supporter of this project from the beginning. In addition I wish to thank Hans Bolliger for the informative lunches, Jacqueline Burckhardt of *Parkett*, Julian Schütt, the great-grandson of Emmy Hennings, and Maria Reinshagen of Christie's, which allowed me to use its marvelous building for a presentation of my research. In Geneva I owe a tremendous debt to Paulo Colombo, Director of the Centre d'Art Contemporain, which mounted a complete survey of my visual work related to Ball, and to the Baroness Lambert for her lively encouragement. In Ticino, I offer thanks to Harald Szeemann, who has long been devoted to Ball studies and whose archives outside Tegna were inspirational. Also, thank you to the dozens of Swiss friends and acquaintances who engaged me in lively conversation about Ball and Dada during my sojourn.

I would like to recognize my collaborators: Donald Baechler, James Brown, John O'Rielly, and not least Kay Rosen and John Baldessari. Thank you, Joel Coleman, for writing so interestingly about my project in your Ph.D. dissertation at the University of Georgia at Athens.

Among curators, I single out the lasting friendship of Gary Garrels, Chief Curator of Drawings at the Museum of Modern Art in New York.

My "Ball" drawings and books are in the hands of many collectors and institutions, and I cannot possibly name them all. I would, however, like to thank Michael and Brenda Sandler, my most loyal friends and colleagues, for their love of art.

Nothing would have transpired without the Matthew Marks Gallery in New York, which represents me. Thank you, Matthew, and thank you, Jeffrey Peabody! To my good friend and editor, Professor Jeffrey T. Schnapp, I doff my hat. It is Jeffrey who helped this book find its home at Yale University Press, and Jeffrey who painstakingly egged on the revision of my manuscript until it evolved into the form you find here. I also thank him for his insightful and intelligent introductory essay. To other friends and family, thank you.

Jonathan Hammer

LIST OF ILLUSTRATIONS

LIST OF ILLUSTRATIONS

x

INTRODUCTION: BALL AND HAMMER

JEFFREY T. SCHNAPP

The conjunction that cements my title rocks like the hobbyhorses in which the book abounds. Its meaning is additive to the degree that the volume is built upon Hugo Ball's visionary novella *Tenderenda the Fantast*, translated and commented upon—both in essay form and through drawings—by the contemporary artist Jonathan Hammer. It is additive also to the degree that Ball plus Hammer equals a portrait of Dada and its legacies at the start of a fresh millennium born under the un-Dada sign of renewed technological optimism. The conjunction seesaws, however, when the equation doesn't neatly balance: owing to the friction between Ball's tortured flight out of time and Hammer's probings of the era of AIDS, to the interpretive vigor and even violence of Hammer's gay use and abuse of the German gnostic, or to the fractures within Ball himself that render *Tenderenda* a purgative work—a peeling away, layer by layer, skin by skin, of his past in the service of the transformation of Ball the Expressionist into Ball the author of *Byzantine Christendom*. Productive imbalances these, that render *Ball and Hammer* a book that is also a puzzle, a rebus whose title tropes Dada's grammar of personified objects. Ball is the plaything and pretext, at once a toy and an aspirant to the spherical resurrected body that Dionysius the Areopagite promised the faithful after the Second Coming. Hammer is the tool that reworks Dada Hugo's self-portrait as that of a contemporary son. The two come together, as if naturally, like ball and chain, ball and socket, ball and peen, hammer and sickle . . . Hammer and Ball.

Jonathan Hammer's engagement with *Tenderenda* stretches back two decades. It matured in 1996, when he was awarded a grant from the Swiss Art Council (Pro Helvetia) in support of a translation and a corpus of drawings that interpret Ball's idiosyncratic autobiographical fiction in what the *New York Times* has referred to as Hammer's mode of "idiosyncratic concentration."[1] Animated by maimed clowns, twisted babies, mutant humanoids, and sadistic toys, the latter works on paper have formed the backbone of several large-format, one-of-a-kind books containing single chapters of *Tenderenda*, bound (as is

1

characteristic of Hammer's bookbindings) in full-leather intaglio covers that feature precious metals and exotic materials such as snakeskin, skate skin, and sharkskin. These images and books have been presented in solo exhibitions in New York, Zurich, Berlin, London, and San Francisco and at the University Art Museum (Berkeley), among other places. A major survey was mounted in 1998 by the Centre d'Art Contemporain in Geneva. *Ball and Hammer* represents the culmination of this decade-long undertaking. By means of a translation of the German original, an essay entitled "Formative Esotericism in Zurich DADA" that effects a speculative queering of Ball, and thirty *Tenderenda*-inspired artworks that at once illustrate the text and translate Ball's imagery into contemporary terms, the present volume proposes a revisionist inquiry into the origins of modernism that is also a revisionist inquiry into postmodern art making.

●

Written between 1914 and 1920, *Tenderenda the Fantast* was to have appeared during Christmas of 1922, accompanied by a suite of woodcuts by Hans Arp. The plan was never realized, and instead the unadorned typescript was left to gather dust until 1967, when it was published posthumously according to the redaction of Annemarie Schütt-Hennings, Ball's stepdaughter. Reissued in 1999 in a revised and annotated edition by Raimund Meyer and Julian Schütt (upon which the present translation is based), *Tenderenda* consists of fifteen chapters that interweave a fractured frame narrative (in the form of an italicized prefatory voice-over describing places such as "Satanopolis" [V] and "The Grand Hotel Metaphysics" [VI]), several loosely connected hallucinatory story lines (concerning characters like Johann the Carousel Horse, Machetanz, Mulche-Mulche, Lilienstein, Laurentius Tenderenda, and Mr. and Mrs. Goldkopf), hymns (often of Latin liturgical inspiration), and incantations like the celebrated noise poems performed by Ball in 1916 on the stage of the Cabaret Voltaire.[2] It is a work whose internal opacities are mirrored by compositional complexities of an external sort. Ball initially referred to it as *Die Phantasten* (The Visionaries) or as his *phantastischer Roman* (fantastic novel) and contemplated subtitles such as *The Eighteen Songs and Paths Through the Realm of the Dead (Die Achtzehn Gesänge und Gänge durchs Totenreich)*. He envisaged its aim as nothing short of a systematic self-dismantling on the part of the author: "the destruction of my hard inner contour," a self-critique "written in advance" carried out by means of a loosely chronological anthology of writings.[3] The result is a work that tracks alongside Ball's memoir from these same years, *Flight Out of Time*, and intervening works like the novella *Flametti, or from the Dandyism of the Poor*

(1918) and the treatise *Towards a Critique of the German Intelligentsia* (1919).[4] *Tenderenda* elaborates upon the same corpus of ideas, materials, and biographical events: Ball's pursuit of a total form of spectacle at the Munich Künstlertheater, his initial enthusiasm and subsequent horrified reaction to World War I, his flight to Zurich, the founding of the Cabaret Voltaire and Galerie Dada, his tense sojourn within the Dada fold, the magic bishop episode, his anarchist sympathies, his deep disaffection with German culture and critique of German idealism, his growing drift toward mysticism, the impact upon his thinking of such figures as Wassily Kandinsky, Richard Huelsenbeck, Ernst Bloch, and especially his wife, Emmy Hennings.[5] But it does so in cryptic fashion.

The adjective *cryptic* is to be taken literally in the case of *Tenderenda*, for in the July 15, 1920, diary entry in which Ball registers the work's completion, he proposes this very similitude:

> I can compare the little book only with that soundly constructed magic chest the old Jews thought Asmodeus was locked in. In all those seven years I have kept on playing with these words and sentences in the midst of torments and doubts. Now the book is finished, and it is a real liberation. I hope that all those fits of malice are buried in it, of which Saint Ambrose says:
>
> Procul recedant somnia
> Et noctium phantasmata,
> Hostemque nostrum comprime.
> [From dreams,
> from nighttime fantasies,
> shield our eyes,
> tread upon our foe.][6]

The liturgical quotation comes from stanza two of the Ambrosian *Te lucis ante* ("before the ending of the day"), minus its concluding phrase, *ne polluantur corpora* ("lest they pollute our bodies"). Pollution is *Tenderenda*'s central theme and serves as the leitmotiv of Hammer's visual-verbal engagement with Ball: pollution as an innate feature of the worlds of history, society, and nature. So innate is pollution that even dreams, fantasies, feverish ferments of the human imagination like the novel itself, in the end, prove no less defiled and defiling than do the harsh and chaotic realities from which they purport to free humankind. The Ball who wrote the above words would have been well aware that the

Te lucis ante was sung by monks at sunset to ward off ill-intentioned phantoms, especially of the sort likely to induce wet dreams.[7] Proof is provided by the comparison of *Tenderenda*'s contents—its torments, doubts, and fits of malice—with the archdevil Asmodeus, king of the demons and genius of conjugal discord, featured in the apocryphal Book of Tobit.[8] The novel thus constitutes itself as an impregnable literary crypt within which are entombed not only Ball's demons—whether Expressionist, Dadaist, sexual, existential, or political—but also Ball himself: the former fantast who, through the exercise of his visionary powers, set out to protest and redeem an inexorably fallen world and who, as a result, found himself corrupted to the bone. The sole alternative ("real liberation") lies outside the confines of sex, reality, or fantasy, which is to say, outside the confines of the novel: namely, in the pristine, supernatural realm inhabited by angels. Seraphic obedience and devotion to God alone can confer upon mortals something akin to a state of beatitude. Locking Nietzsche's Dionysius and his fleshly retinue of demons inside its soundly constructed chest, *Tenderenda* gestures silently, beyond itself, in the direction of a truer Dada: Dionysius the Areopagite. "When I came across the word *dada*," Ball recalled in 1921, "I was called upon twice by Dionysius. D.A.—D.A."[9]

Half a decade would pass before Ball responded to this double call, although the mere fact that the call can be traced back to his days in Zurich suggests that *Tenderenda* may be a crypt but that it is far from dead and its contents are alive with magic. Demons possess genuine power within Ball's Manichaean belief system.[10] So do the words and sentences played with during seven years of "torments and doubts." Ball the fantast's pursuit of magical alternatives to what he dismissed as "secondhand writing," writing either as denatured by philosophers or as corrupted by journalists and literary naturalists, subservient to and imitative of reality, places him in the company of a wide array of contemporary linguistic dreamers, including spiritists, poets (Velimir Khlebnikov), and speculative semioticians (Ferdinand de Saussure the anagrammatist, Ernest Fenellosa, Ezra Pound). Ball envisaged himself as a rediscoverer of "the evangelical concept of the word (logos) as a magical complex image," which is to say, of a visionary, generative mode of expression that, tapping the innermost alchemical powers of the word, renders unfamiliar worlds familiar by means of semantic units that are simultaneously words, pictures, and incantations.[11] The pioneer had been the Italian Futurist Marinetti, whose words-in-freedom poems were composed not of conventional words but of "polyexpressive" signs: polyexpressive because they were infinitely combinable, contractable, and expansible according to the principles of lyrical analogy, "free expressive orthography," and onomatopoeia; polyexpressive also because, liberated from the prison house of syntax, they were free to operate within a hybrid poetic space at once constructed like a visual tableau and like a script for live performance and improvisation.[12] The space in question was one in which information would no longer be relayed at a comfortable distance or speed but rather would immerse audiences in the particulars of a given scene from a dizzying multiplicity of perspectives, from the heavens to the action of molecules to externalia (lists, road signs, telegrams, telephone calls, noises) to sounds, thoughts, images, and analogies emanating like machine-gun fire from the lyric sensibility of the poet-performer. Marinetti's aims were hypermimetic—a kind of lyrical shock journalism in which every word packs a literal punch or slap, driven home by means of a boisterous live performance. But Ball rightly perceived a deeper, transverbal and transmimetic urge: to restore to the poetic word its presemantic, prerational force; to close the gap between sign and referent; to anoint the poet once again as a literal maker of worlds, a magician, a priest, a conjurer of elemental energies. Little did it matter that, aside from anti-Germanism and scorn for Enlightenment ideals, Ball shared few of Marinetti's beliefs, namely, his acritical celebration of modern industry, his cult of speed and mechanized war, his intransigent nationalism.

On the coattails of Futurism's revolution in poetic language, Ball explored the same paradoxical verbal-visual-vocal territory in *Tenderenda*'s opening chapters: "little sections of four to five pages each, in which I practice discipline of language and try at the same time to preserve some remnant of serenity."[13] These early efforts, bearing titles such as "The Rise of the Seer" (I), "Johann the Carousel Horse" (II) and "The Decline of the Dance Maker" (III), were performed in public readings at the Cabaret Voltaire and the Zurich Zunfthaus zur Zimmerleuten in late 1915 and early 1916. Alternately oracular and childish, always intended for purposes of performance, they were followed by Ball's turn in mid-1916 to the celebrated *Verse ohne Worte* (wordless lyrics) or *Lautgedichte* (sound poems) that he chanted in the style of priestly lamentations from the stage of the Cabaret Voltaire, dressed in a cylinder of shiny blue cardboard like a magic bishop.[14] Two such compositions are featured in *Tenderenda*, both from the *gadji beri bimba* cycle: "Jolifanto bamblo ô falli bamblo" (XI) and "Baubo sbugi ninga gloffa" (XIV). The wordless lyric took the Futurist destruction of syntax one step further (or rather, deeper): "We tried to give the isolated vocables the fullness of an oath, the glow of a star. And curiously enough, the magically inspired vocables conceived and gave birth to a *new* sentence that was not limited and confined by any conventional meaning. Touching lightly on a hundred ideas at the same time without naming them, this sentence made it possible to hear the innately playful, but hidden, irrational character of the listener; it wakened and strengthened the lowest strata of memory."[15] Vocalization was for Ball the precondition for semantic fullness, a plenitude emblematized by oaths, hymns, prayers, poems, and prophetic utterances (including worshipful silence, incantations, and glossolalia). All are bulwarks against the unvoiced forms of expression practiced by journalists and idealist philosophers.[16] But how to get beyond the old sentence with its confining nouns and names? By means of a childlike poetics founded upon *nonsense* and *noise*, or rather, the interweaving of neologism and incantation. "Noises (an *rrrr* drawn out for minutes, or crashes, or sirens, etc.)," Ball wrote in his diary on March 30, 1916, thinking of such works as Marinetti's *Zang Tumb Tumb*, "are superior to the human voice in energy."[17] Elemental energies are restored to the human voice when it regains its role as noisemaker. For Marinetti, this meant crosscutting real-world noises, conveyed in onomatopoeic fashion, with the momentary effluvium of a lyric subject taking hold of and placing his imprint upon the kaleidoscopic reality of the event. For Ball, this meant a serious form of play in which the performer is transformed into a sorcerer and the listener is plunged beneath the semantic level of language into the primeval recesses of human memory.

Noises and chants are one solution to rescuing human language from emptiness and corruption. Words that touch lightly on a hundred ideas at the same time without naming them definitively are another: invented words like *blago bung blago bung* (XI, ll. 7–8), evocative at once of the sound of marching elephants and of cognates for swelling bellies (*blähen*), drums (*bongos*), and practical jokes (*blagues*).[18] Existing words like *Dada*, defined in *Flight Out of Time* as "yes, yes" in Romanian, as "rocking horse" and "hobbyhorse" in French, and as "a sign of foolish naïveté, joy in procreation, and preoccupation with the baby carriage" in German.[19] Subsequent scholarship has laid bare additional layers of reference in the case of this most enduring of Ball's magic words: for example, to a hair tonic manufactured by the maker also of a lily-milk soap. This helps to make sense of certain, otherwise obscure phrases in the First Dada Manifesto, like "Dada is the world's best lily-milk soap . . . Dada Mr. Anastasius Lilienstein."[20] But what of the manifesto's repeated assertions that eternal bliss can be achieved by reciting mantras like *dada m'dada dada m'dada dada mhm* "until one loses consciousness" and that "Dada is the world soul" and "Dada the heart of words"?[21] Are they to be understood as tomfoolery or as metaphysical bombast or, rather, as tomfoolery with a serious metaphysical purpose? Here the reader would do well to consider the novel hypothesis, advanced in Hammer's essay and encoded in his bookbinding for *Three Rings for Hildegarde*, that Ball equated the word *Dada* with the Hebrew letters that make up the holy name *Yahweh*: "Ball conceived of DADA as a password, as a way to attain access to the ineffable through meditation, as a Kabalistic method (uninformed by actual Kabalistic doctrine) to further his vigorous work of prophecy, self-sacrifice, and cultural healing."[22] The claim, of course, is unprovable. What is certain is that Ball's revolt against materialism and economic reason bred early sympathies for the Berlin Orient (despite occasional anti-Semitic rages, usually as anti-German as they are anti-Semitic).[23] It must also have prompted readings from the biblical Apocrypha and pseudepigrapha, the hermetic corpus, and from various Judaic, pre-Christian, and Neoplatonic mystical traditions, to judge by the traces scattered across the pages of *Tenderenda*. The strength of Hammer's revisitation of these traces resides in the speculative vigor with which he assembles them into an esoteric interpretation of Zurich Dada as a whole.

The interpretation in question is often persuasive. At other times it is selective (for instance, downplaying *Tenderenda*'s extensive borrowings from the liturgy and the Church Fathers). At other times it is more about Hammer than Ball. Yet Hammer's study rightly draws attention to a domain neglected by cultural historians: namely, the sustained contacts between the early avant-gardes and esoteric groups, from spiritists, table rappers, and students of automatic writing and ectoplastic flows; to enthusiasts of Egyptian magic, Chaldean religion and Kabala; to influential communities that included dancers (Mary Wigman, Isadora Duncan), artists, and metaphysicians close to the Dada fold, which assembled in Ascona, Switzerland, around Rudolph Von Laban, the Hungarian choreographer, at Monte Verità (Mountain of Truth).[24] Evidence of the impact of such encounters is not hard to come by. In the case of Futurism, suffice it to recall Anton Giulio Bragaglia's efforts to photograph the auralike emanations of human bodies that form a continuum with his later "foto-dynamic" portraits of bodies in motion; or Marinetti's long-standing conviction that radio waves were vibrations issuing forth "from living or dead spirits."[25] Nor was Ball the only gnostic to pass in and out of the Dada fold, for Julius Evola followed a not dissimilar course. A fierce critic of contemporary industrial civilization, Evola renounced Dadaism in 1923 in favor of the study of alchemy, gnosticism, and Asian philosophy and went on to become the proponent of a hermetic brand of fascism built around notions of "spiritual racism" and "pagan imperialism."[26] The examples of Bragaglia, Marinetti, and Evola (to which one might add a far longer list of names extending from Giovanni Papini to Antonin Artaud to

Yukio Mishima) confirm the significance of the wing of modernism that, in the course of its work of cultural demolition and construction, sought total and even totalitarian alternatives to Enlightenment reason, whether Western or non-Western, orthodox or esoteric, backward- or forward-looking, or a combination of the above.[27] They also suggest that, for all its apparent eccentricity, Ball's flight out of time was not so eccentric after all.

Ball's musings on magic words and verbal tactics in *Tenderenda* are difficult to disentangle from his emerging fascination with Dionysius's treatise *On the Divine Names*. Although an absolutely singular being, God possesses a multitude of names, writes the sixth-century Neoplatonist. Each is "true" and endowed with power. But not one of these predicates fully encompasses His glory or power. The same might be said in a ludic key of the legion of masks donned by Ball in the course of his book. Each is "true" and each reveals a stratum of his being. Ball is the unnamed "author" who comments in advance upon the contents of each chapter. Ball is the seer-trickster who mesmerizes the mob with his enchanted magnifying glass in the opening chapter. Ball is the journalist Lilienstein (*Lilien* + *Stein* = stone lilies) persecuted by the inhabitants of Satanopolis. Ball is the Roasted Poet offered up as a sacrificial victim to an army of ghosts at the end of Chapter VII: "a hermaphrodite from head to toe . . . his head a wonderful onion of spirituality."[28] Most especially, Ball is the titular hero Laurentius Tenderenda, the childlike church poet "spat up" by the narrative in Chapter XIII. Shy and retiring, fatigued by Dada's destructive mirth, Laurentius has been tenderized by the wanton horrors and wonders in which the text abounds. His sole longing is for the blessings of heaven as befits a being whose name is borrowed from a favorite martyr: Saint Lawrence.

The story of the third-century Spanish archdeacon deeply moved the nine-year-old Ball, as he attests in *Flight Out of Time*: "When I was nine years old and heard the story of Saint Lawrence, I came close to fainting. With great effort I corrupted myself; I tried to adapt myself. To my timid nature, brutality was enticing. I tried as hard as I could to cast off the nobler, tenderer sentiments. And thus enthusiasms became perversions."[29] Lawrence's is a characteristically jumbled hagiography, blending cruelty and ecstasy, the sublime and the comic, history and hallucination, much like *Tenderenda* itself. The medieval version redacted by Jacobus de Voragine begins with an evocative etymology: Laurentius derives from *lauream tenens*, or "he who holds the laurel wreath," because victorious in his passion, Lawrence "softens the hardened heart, restores the hearing of the spirit, and wards off the lightning of the sentence of the damned."[30] Next comes the usual succession of saintly acts and accompanying torments: Lawrence distributes Caesar's treasure to the poor and is imprisoned by the tyrant Decius; he cures the blind and converts others in the course of his imprisonment, for which Decius accuses him of practicing magic; threatened with tortures, Lawrence proclaims his indifference to physical suffering: "My night has no darkness: all things shine with light!"[31] In return for this and other expressions of faith, Lawrence is splayed on a gridiron over a bed of burning coals and prodded with iron forks, becoming the culinary double of Christ stretched out on the cross, the roasted saint upon whom is modeled Ball's Roasted Poet. The scene involves elements of Eucharistic parody even in the version preserved in the current liturgy for Lawrence's saint's day. The victim offers cooking instructions from the gridiron and incites his tormentor-cook to partake of his flesh: "Behold, wretch, you have well cooked one side! Turn the other, and eat!"[32] Decius passes, and Lawrence gives up the ghost. Anointed with spices, his charred body is buried the following day, amid the tears and lamentations of the faithful. That Ball's Latin neologism *tenderenda* plays off of a multitude of details from this tale should be self-evident. The coinage is based upon *tendenda*, the gerundive nominative singular feminine form of the verb *tendo* (to extend, to stretch out, to strive, to exert oneself in opposition), which could be roughly translated as "she to be extended."[33] To arrive at *tenderenda*, Ball interpolates the syllable *-er* between the verb stem *tend-* and the suffix *-enda*. In so doing, he echoes the adjective *tener*, the root word from which is derived the English word *tender*, whose Latin meanings include "softness," "delicacy," "effeminacy," and "youth." All this to arrive at a hermaphroditic proper name that signifies something like Lawrence (m.) Softly-to-be-extended (f.).

An attentive reader of *Flight Out of Time* may rightly wonder about the word game's pertinence to the diary's assertion that every genius is endowed with the gift of sexual changeability: the protean capacity to shuttle back and forth between male and female stances.[34] Indeed, Neoplatonic myths of cosmic restoration and turn-of-the-century theories of artistic creation had assigned a key role to hermaphroditism. But what Ball refers to in his diary as the "hermaphroditic element" represents only one facet of a broader thematics of self-multiplication linked, in turn, to spiritual growth and self-overcoming through a process of self-softening that is at once forward- and backward-looking: "Man has many egos, just as the onion has many skins. It is not a matter of one ego more or less. The center is still made of skins. It is astonishing to see how tenaciously man holds onto his prejudices. He endures the harshest torture merely to avoid surrendering himself. The most tender, innermost being of man must be very sensitive; but it is without doubt also very wonderful. Few people attain this insight and notion; because they fear for the vulnerability of their soul. Fear precludes reverence."[35] The paradox is deliberate and essential to understanding *Tenderenda*. The center of the self is no center at all. It contains further skins, further masks, further layers of growth. There exists, nonetheless, a hypothetical center, associated with regression to those "nobler, tenderer sentiments" of childhood that socialization has buried under the armor-plated contours of the ego. But this center ultimately lies not in the past but in the future: in a form of selfless selfhood, ultrasensitive and ultravulnerable, open to union with the divine. Laurentius Tenderenda is therefore a name that harks back to and marks the recovery of that delicate nine-year-old moved to fainting by the tale of the Roman martyr's ordeal. At the same time, Laurentius Tenderenda designates yet another momentary self-extension toward a "reverence" to come: the condition of seraphic tenderness that lies behind and beyond the procession of veils that makes up Ball's *phantastischer Roman.*

●

Tenderenda's oracular style and proliferation of authorial masks render it a capacious and obscure text. The absence of Arp's woodcuts also makes it an incomplete one. Jonathan Hammer's efforts to inhabit and develop this capaciousness, obscurity, and incompletion began with a series of one-of-a-kind volumes that he handcrafted in the early 1990s.[36] Bearing such titles as *Satanopolis, Three Rings for Hildegarde,* and *The Violet-Faced Seer,* each contains a small fragment of an English version of the German original, in effect, prying apart the autobiographical fable that Ball strove so hard to piece together. Each is accompanied by a body of drawings, sometimes related (at times only obliquely so) to Ball's text; some are drawn by Hammer, some by collaborators such as John Baldessari, Donald Baechler, James Brown, John O'Reilly, and Kay Rosen. Each volume functions as a "cover" in the musical sense: an updating that appropriates, encroaches upon, and supplants its modernist model. Each performs this triple action by encasing text and illustrations in one of Hammer's signature book covers: lavish intaglio compositions of embossed leather, parchment, and metal leaf that at once repel and attract the viewer through their meticulous sense of craft, vivid chromatics, and the tactile properties of materials like vellum, snakeskin, and eel skin. The resulting object is enigmatic. Sumptuous and exclusive but willfully teetering on the edge of tawdriness or vampiness, pretending not to circulate but packaged as a luxury commodity, it hypes Ball as it buries him in a soundly constructed postmodern *Wunderkammer* in which the magic within has become that of a cosmic and comic carny show. Hammer's books summon their viewer to step right up: not to read but to judge them by their cover. One cover overwrites Ball with an exchange of letters on *Tenderenda* between Hammer and Rosen. Another reads *John Baldessari & Jonathan Hammer Present the Decline of the Dance Maker by Hugo Ball* juxtaposed with the trademark image of Zurich Dada: Ball dressed as the magic bishop on the stage of the Cabaret Voltaire. But in place of Dada Hugo's face looms a hole.

Behind the hole lurks the face of an invisible clown, which is to say, of Hammer himself clowning around in his drawings. The clown in question has been reared on a heady mix of Hollywood glitz and readings from Hermes Trismegistus, medieval alchemy, Dante, Giordano Bruno, the marquis de Sade, Rudolph Steiner, Sigmund Freud, and Georges Bataille. He long ago abandoned that family of predecessors drawn from the world of circuses and popular entertainments in whom modern artists from Lautrec to Picasso and Gris to Klee sought a mirror in which to reflect upon their own condition as the wandering minstrels of the age of industry. A melancholy mirror because these contortionists, tightrope walkers, bearded ladies, dwarfs, and harlequins may hover about on the inner or outer edge of cities, outside the realm of production as work, inside the arena of production as play, but they are never reducible to mere toys. Rather, like the modern artist, they emit a halo, the aura-aureole borne by Baudelaire's poet in *Mon coeur mis à nu*, theoretically gilded by Walter Benjamin. The halo of human dignity.

Nothing could be further from the gleeful defacements carried out in Hammer's work on Ball, which take their cue from the latter's abiding ambivalence toward vaudevillians. For the founder of the Cabaret Voltaire, these precarious beings, on the one hand, stand as the sole upholders of human values in an era of standardization and mechanization; on the other, they represent an alternative that is no alternative at all, because in the course of both *Tenderenda* and *Flametti,* they prove every bit as crass and inhumane as the society against which they rise in revolt. Hammer's circus stylings broaden the vector of disenchantment and, like those of Bruce Naumann, they leave nary a trace of a halo in sight. The amusement park and the cabaret have been infested by AIDS. The circus has been taken over by baby batterers and buggerers. The minstrel show has become a con. The pale cobalt luster of Picasso's harlequin, Gris's geometrical grisaille, Klee's sappy decorativism give way to metallic shards, flaking off like the scabs of lesions, on the faces of Hammer's clowns and the bodies of his ravaged rag dolls. Victims and victimizers at the same time, all they want is to turn a quick trick—by leading the blind down a blind alleyway, by pulling the wool over someone's eyes, by flashing their private parts, by hacking their donkey partner to bits. Theirs is a comic-apocalyptic world akin to that inhabited by *Tenderenda*'s tricksters, but in the place of Ball's intimations of future reverence there appear only fragments of a system of private reference.

To Hammer's esoteric reading of Zurich Dada corresponds the hermetic coding of some of his most remarkable *Tenderenda*-inspired images. Take, as a case in point, his drawing *The Violet-Faced Seer*, an emblem (in the Renaissance sense of the word) based upon the description in Ball's opening chapter of a charlatan who appears in the marketplace to expound his ideas about an impending rapture but fails to persuade owing to public skepticism. The connection between text and image hinges on a magnifying glass held "aloft in tragic pose," according to *Tenderenda:* "tragic" because the glass is about to shatter and its splinters are about to lacerate the world. In Hammer's version, the glass hangs perilously upside down from the barely prehensile spatulated hand of a creature whose lower extremities are at once reptilian and hydralike. The trunk is that of a human hermaphrodite. A solitary fin sprouts from behind the left scapula. In the place of the face there is a hole: not the blank visage of a Dada bishop but the wound left behind by a severed head, a red ball, the nose of a clown, a displaced genital orifice. Hovering behind in the form of a sectioned lotus root is a pair of violet eyes and the attenuated violet "face" of the prophet who denounced humanity as "a chimera, a wonder, a godly approximate, filled with scheming forethought and deceit."[37] Extending above him as if an outcropping of his brain matter is a lush coral reef of fantasies, dreams, and thoughts.[38]

The Seer rises up unmoored against a plain backdrop, as if the gaseous emanation of the (pineal) eye of a book, itself issuing forth from a Sphinx who is barely sketched out. The riddle of the picture is thus connected with the riddle of the Sphinx, but the answer ("man") remains riddlelike inasmuch as the being in question figures as an unstable composite of male and female, reptile and human, vapor and flesh—spirit, spit, and shit. Here and elsewhere in Hammer's imagination, the instability is present at birth. Inhabiting a universe cast in the image of a serpent that bites its own tail, humankind is caught in a phylogenetic time loop such that evolution is always bidirectional, always equal to devolution. The ontogenetic corollary bears even greater weight: aging too is bidirectional, always equal to regression—which is why the clowns under Hammer's big top assume the form of infant-elders.

Late antiquity devised various names for such a hybrid creature, prominent among them the παιδαριογέρων, or *puer senex* (boy–old man), celebrated by Christian authors from the hagiographers of the Eastern Church to Gregory the Great to Alan of Lille. For them, as for their pagan predecessors, the infant-elder represented an ethical ideal: wisdom and prudence combined with innocence and purity.[39] In Hammer's chamber of post-Dada wonders and horrors, ancient ideals perform a cartwheel. Senile dementia and disease invade the playpen; infancy is sexed like a dirty old man; adults are crybabies; babies serve as ringleaders. Such is the case, for instance, in *Landscape from the Upper Inferno.* The title refers the viewer to the opening section of Chapter IV of *Tenderenda,* entitled "The Red Heavens": "Landscape from the upper inferno. A concert of great cacophonous noises that astonish even the animals. The animals appear, some as musicians caterwauling, some in the embalmed state of a diorama. The aunties from the seventh dimension participate obscenely in the witches' Sabbath." Hammer's visual interpretation dovetails with the speculative outing of Ball proposed in "Formative Esotericism in Zurich DADA." Both depend upon a careful teasing out of the passage's Dantean cues. The "seventh dimension" (*siebenten Dimension*) is understood as the seventh circle of Dante's upper Hell, whose third and final subcircle subjects the violent against God, Nature, and industry to an eternal rain of fire. Among the violent against Nature are the sodomites, with whom Hammer conflates the rampaging "aunties" (*Tante*) alluded to above. He conflates their representative-in-chief, Dante's teacher, the poet-philosopher Brunetto Latini, with Laurentius Tenderenda, which is to say with one of the ego skins of Dada Hugo. The coupling clicks because, like Lawrence on the gridiron and *Tenderenda*'s Roasted Poet, Brunetto is literally "browned" by the infernal flames (in a pun on his name, which means "little brown one").[40] Brunetto is also associated with stretching, with the "ill distended muscles" that he and his sodomitical peers left behind them at the moment of death.[41] And he is the builder of his own soundly constructed literary crypt: the *Treasure* (*Tesoro*). "Let my *Treasure* be commended to you, in which I live still, and I ask no more" are Brunetto's parting words—this in a canto built upon reversals of the natural hierarchy between teacher and pupil, old and young, top and bottom, head and foot, time and eternity.[42]

The Ball-Dante connections may seem oblique, but oblique or not, they provide the interpretive framework needed to make sense of circus pictures such as *Landscape from the Upper Inferno.* The "landscape" offered up here is fleshly: three male infant clowns, two wearing top hats, the third headless, caterwauling as they cavort, perhaps as "aunties from the seventh dimension." The red disks on their faces bespeak the artificial cheer and glow of pancake makeup. They are signs of play (maybe even of contemplative play); but they are also wounds, wounds that bleed and call to memory the severed head of the Violet-Faced Seer. The conjunction of cruelty, humor, and play is cemented by the toys that proliferate in Hammer's work. Pinwheels, whirligigs, carts, hoops, dolls, wagons, hobbyhorses, jack-in-the-boxes, these are just a few of the playthings whose innocent surfaces belie their true identity as hellish instruments of torture and sadistic pleasure. Two pinwheels appear in the upper portion of *Landscape.* One gently slashes across the neck of a top-hat toting infant, as if to choke him. The other plunges down from above the picture plane like a twisting branding iron and binds the upper edge. Two hobbyhorses accompany them, seeming to penetrate the caterwaulers' bodies. In each case there is a disjunction between the horse's head and the canelike extension. The former swings free toward the front, in one case suggestively swooshing out of a baby's genitals; the latter vanishes, no less suggestively, into their rumps. Other images, like *Jumping Jack with His Nose in His Hand* (also present on the cover of *Three Rings for Hildegard*), as well as the anus on the headless tumbling infant pointed at the viewer, confirm that, in Hammer's version of the aunties of upper Hell, it is the hobbyhorse that rides the rider, not the rider the horse.

Such reversals are the rule in Hammer's topsy-turvy toy stories. In *Goat Pushing Clown,* the cart precedes the horse, or rather, a hapless clown teeters atop a cart being pushed (or mounted) by a goat. The first bears the usual red dots (or are they pox?); the second, a red belt, the mark that he has been singled out as a scapegoat. Wheels sprout from bodies (*Pull Me*), legs and arms recede into bellies (*Push Me*), boxes box Jack into his proverbial box (*Boxed In #2*), swaggering dancers are transformed into foot-actuated jointed dummies (*Machetanz*, the dance maker, is made to dance), hands lose their grasp on the world and are either spatulated or truncated (*Zirritig-Zirrizitig, Mulche-Mulche in Labor*), in what adds up to a universal loss of agency. In Hammer's end-of-the-century translation of Ball's apocalypticism, the human is reduced to the status of plaything, the plaything is raised to the status of the human, and the playpen is portrayed as a toy-eat-toy world.

Toys have always provided a privileged lens through which to examine a civilization. Once mere by-products of craft fabrication, in the course of the first and second Industrial Revolutions toys increased in scale, complexity, and realism, underwent standardization and specialization, and emerged as mass-produced commodities. They gave rise to an autonomous industry precisely as industrial societies began to confer the status of autonomy upon childhood itself and to situate play outside the compass of instrumental reason. Play was increasingly thought of as a disinterested activity (like aesthetic play in Kant's *Third Critique*), and toys, for all their practical value as agents of socialization, were designed to provide evasion and entertainment, not immersion in the world. Progressive educators and modern design movements rejected the decoupling of play from acting in or upon the world. They devised new process-oriented toys like modular building blocks, Mecanos, Assemblos, Erector sets, Legos, and the like—toys that were functional in nature, used modern materials, and made use of primary colors and forms.[43] Play was to become the expression of a child's inventive powers and a means for forging a new humanity, informed by the functionalist and rationalist ideals of the architect-engineer. Hammer's toys are decidedly neither these modern(ist) educational toys nor the escapist toys that preceded them. Culled from the museum of pre- or proto-industrial playthings, not unrelated to Hans Bellmer's articulated dolls, they represent deliberate throwbacks to a primal scene of play. Many are folk toys closely related to folktales, with histories stretching back to antiquity and forward to contemporary county fairs. Some are relics of the eighteenth century, remembered only by toy collectors, historians, and readers of Laurence Sterne's *Tristram Shandy* (namely, Toby the hobby); others are archaeological specimens. All are the products of a craft tradition. But a craft tradition that has been altered, *detourné* (bent in purpose and use value), even mutilated by means of Hammer's own image-making craft. No toy survives the process of adaptation intact. Jumping jacks lose their noses, and where one leg is erased, a prosthetic limb torn from another appears (at the expense of symmetry and bodily cohesion). Jointed dolls "dance" without a pelvis, hands, or feet. Personified whirligigs appear whirled into a daze. Hypercephalic clowns are hung on the white page. At their most complex (the *Transforming Hobbyhorse* series), folk toys find themselves twisted by Hammer into objects that recall the elaborate systems of bodily restraint devised in the name of children's physical and moral hygiene by enlightened reformers like Doctor Daniel Gottlieb Moritz Schreber in the first half of the nineteenth century. Such devices recur but viewed from the skewed perspective of Schreber *fils*, the celebrated subject of Freud's 1911 *Psychoanalytic Notes upon an Autobiographical Account of a Case of Paranoia (Dementia Paranoides)*.[44] They return as infernal machinery implicated in the formation of a hallucinatory dysfunctional body alternately lacking in lungs, intestines, a stomach, an esophagus, as a body feminized by God so that its sphincter may redeem the world.

If there is a single toy, a toy of toys, that best sums up the conjunction of Ball and Hammer, it is the one with which this essay began: the hobbyhorse or carousel horse. *Tenderenda*'s principal hobbyhorse bears the name Johann (an ironic nod in the direction of Goethe). Johann is the passive protagonist of Chapter II, though he resurfaces later in the prison curses of Machetanz and alongside the purring aunties of "The Red Heavens" in the couplet

> The clay pigeon falls from the roof.
> The doubled Johann springs for it up on his hoofs.

From the outset, Ball proclaims Johann no ordinary hobby horse. He is designated as the symbol and idol of the "sterilized visionary club of the Blue Tulip," a community of expressionist poets, clownlike because they sport celluloid noses; this group anticipates the outbreak of World War I and transports him to safety in Libya during the summer of 1914.[45] Johann is wadded in cotton wool and led by a leash across the desert until the visionary company is intercepted by Chieftain Feuerschein (*Feuer* = fire; *Schein* = glow), a fire-eating vaudeville impresario in *Flametti* recast here as a police informant. The chapter closes as Feuerschein detains them for keeping the hobbyhorse from "performing his military duties." In short, the chapter serves up the usual encrypted mix of high seriousness and silliness, autobiographical fact and extravagant fiction. So what sort of object is Johann? *Tenderenda* suggests that he is at once a toy horse, a "real" horse, and an emblem of fantasy—sterile fantasy that transports elsewhere but leads nowhere. The members of the Blue Tulip ride him to flee the polluted world of the Hegelian "thing in itself," the "therefores" and "contrasts" of legal discourse, the walls and wars erected by nation-states, the paddy wagons of Chieftain Feuerschein. But what Johann precipitates is not escape but repetition. Even when detached from the merry-go-round that, in turn, transports him, the carousel horse returns the rider to the desert landscape in which the journey began.

Hammer retains Johann's association with circularity but strips him of the particulars that make *Tenderenda* a memoir of Ball's season in Hell. In so doing Hammer brings to the foreground a background element in Ball: namely, desire—(homo)sexual desire; the desire to extend, complete, or alter the self by prosthetic means; the desire for pleasure, possession, and domination. Such a recoding of Johann is consistent with the philological record. Long before the word *hobby* came to designate the pastimes cultivated by modern subjects as an expression of their individuality, the term referred both to actual ponies and to the wickerwork representations of them worn by morris dancers. Other meanings were not long in coming. The hobbyhorse became not only a toy encompassing everything from a stick with a horse's head to, later, the wooden

INTRODUCTION

16

horses mounted on merry-go-rounds but also a phrase referring to antic performers such as jesters and clowns, as well as to voluptuaries, prostitutes, and loose women. Hence, the offended question "Call'st thou my love 'hobby-horse'?" in Shakespeare's *Love's Labor's Lost* (3.1.26). Hammer's hobbies are also toy horses, "real" horses, and emblems of fantasy. Fantasy, however, is now decoupled from poetic vision and linked to libidinal drives that are "sterile" to the degree that they are nonreproductive. The 1995 drawing *Johann the Carousel Horse* illustrates my point. Not unlike *Lunetz's Leg Clad in Rose-Colored Silk*, it plants Emmy Hennings's smiling head atop a pair of dancing female legs, truncated in such a fashion that the right rotates counterclockwise on its toe and the left is pressed down laterally into and under the genitals of a hinged infant-dummy enclosed by a circular railing mounted on the tail end of Johann. The latter has been deprived of wheels. He has been reduced to a spring-mounted half-seesaw, reminiscent of the foot-actuated Machetanz. The infant-dummy's gender is impossible to determine, but two things are certain: his or her extremities have been maimed yet again, and (s)he is being maneuvered like a puppet. Johann's "rider" and, by extension, Johann himself are both being "ridden" by the towering Hennings, whose head encroaches upon and completes the headless body of a toddler whose identity is on loan. Is the picture an emblem of the fully tenderized, castrated post-Dada Ball, under the spell of Hennings's fervent brand of Catholicism? Or does it obliquely figure Hammer's own art of self-invention and self-promotion through his appropriation of and encroachment upon Ball? Or is it instead an allegory of Johann-Jonathan the contemporary artist prompted by the art world to play the clown and to furnish visionary rides that foster illusions of fullness and fulfillment where, in reality, there is only hollowness and hype? Or is it all of the above? A reply may be gleaned from one last drawing, *Self-Portrait as Hobbyhorse,* where the hobby figures as a rocking horse. Its body is skeletal, fleshed out only by a worn seat and a tattered neck cloth. Its head beckons as the only solid volume. Lifted out of the pages of a catalogue of old toys, the horse projects the wide-eyed innocence of a child, as if it were simply longing to fulfill its destiny: waiting to sweetly rock and be rocked. Yet two details belie its innocence and passivity: a red ball nose affiliates the artist-qua-hobbyhorse with the trickster clowns of Hammer's circus. A forked tongue mocks and threatens the very beholder being seduced into embarking on a journey to nowhere. The moral of this and every one of Hammer's hobbyhorses is paradoxical: namely, that the world of objects never ceases to talk back to the world of subjects and vice versa. In *Ball and Hammer* the conversation extends across twentieth-century art.

NOTES

1 "Also of Note: Critic's Choices," *New York Times*, November 25, 1994, C-24.

2 The first edition was published by Verlag der Arche in Zurich and translated into English by Malcolm Green in *Blago Bung Blago Bung Bosso Fataka! The First Texts of German Dada: Hugo Ball—Richard Huelsenbeck—Walter Serner* (London: Atlas Books, 1995); the second revised edition, edited by Raimond Meyer and Julian Schütt, was published by Haymon in Innsbruck. My annotations to *Tenderenda* rely both upon the Meyer-Schütt edition and upon Green. In "Dada Dances: Hugo Ball's *Tenderenda der Phantast*," Siegbert Prawer has suggested that Ball's prefaces are modeled after those in Boccaccio or eighteenth-century English novels. See P. F. Ganz, ed., *The Discontinuous Tradition: Studies in Honor of Ernest Ludwig Stahl* (Oxford: Clarendon Press, 1971), 212.

3 Hugo Ball, *Flight Out of Time: A Dada Diary*, ed. John Elderfield, trans. Ann Raimes (Berkeley: University of California Press, 1996), 83.

4 Hugo Ball, *Flametti oder Vom Dandysmus der Armen* (Berlin: Reiss, 1918; rpt. Frankfurt: Suhrkamp, 1975) has never been translated into English; *Towards a Critique of the German Intelligentsia* exists in a recent English translation by Brian L. Harris (New York: Columbia University Press, 1993).

5 There are two recent overall studies of Ball's life and writings in English: Philip Mann, *Hugo Ball: An Intellectual Biography*, Bithell Series of Dissertations 13 (London: Institute for Germanic Studies, 1987); and Erdmute Wenzel White, *The Magic Bishop: Hugo Ball, Dada Poet*, Studies in German Literature, Linguistics and Culture (Columbia, S.C.: Camden House, 1998). There also exists an excellent exhibition catalogue covering all phases of his biography entitled *Hugo Ball (1886–1986): Leben und Werk*, ed. Ernst Teubner (Berlin: Publica, 1986); and a full bibliography, also by Teubner, *Hugo Ball: Eine Bibliographie*, Bibliographische Hefte 1 (Mainz: Hase & Koehler, 1992). The best interpretive commentary on *Tenderenda* is Claudia Rechner-Zimmermann's *Die Flucht in die Sprache: Hugo Ball's Phantastenroman im kulturgeschichtlichen Kontext zwischen 1914 und 1920* (Marburg: Hitzeroth, 1992), but Green's introduction and notes to *Blago Bung Blago Bung Bosso Fataka!* are also worth consulting.

6 Ball, *Flight Out of Time*, 186–87. The translation of Ambrose's hymn is mine.

7 Indeed, in the *Divine Comedy*, the pilgrims on the slopes of Purgatory sing out precisely this hymn (canto 8, v. 13) in the Valley of the Princes, so as to ward off dreams like the homoerotic rape-rapture endured by Dante himself in the following canto. As indicated later in the essay, Ball was a highly attentive reader of Dante.

8 Sometimes identified with Beelzebub, Asmodeus is the protagonist of the story of Sarah, whose beauty so enchants him that he slays each of her seven husbands on the night of their nuptials. The tale is recounted in the Book of Tobit (3.8) and concludes with an exorcism: Tobias incinerates the heart and liver of a fish, driving off Asmodeus to Egypt. Asmodeus, however, reappears in several Talmudic stories involving Solomon.

9 Ball, *Flight Out of Time*, 210. The entry is dated June 18, 1921.

10 Here Ball is consistent with Patristic belief. One of Ball's favorite Patristic authors, Augustine, had argued in his *City of God* in favor of the existence of demons, the proof of their existence being the efficacy of magic.

11 Ball, *Flight Out of Time*, 68. In his essay, Hammer explores the Kabalistic resonances of this exploration of alternate forms of "writing."

12 See Ball, *Flight Out of Time*, 68: "With the sentence having given way to the word, the circle around Marinetti began resolutely with *parole in libertà*. They took the work out of the sentence frame (the word image) that had been thoughtlessly and automatically assigned to it, nourished the emaciated big-city vocables with light and air, and gave them back their warmth, emotion, and their original untroubled freedom." On Marinetti's words-in-freedom poetics, see Jeffrey T. Schnapp, "From Poetics to Politics," *Stanford Italian Review* 5.1 (1985): 75–92; for a comparative study of Marinetti, Ball, and Carl Einstein (the author of another model text entitled *Bebuquin*), see Rechner-Zimmermann, *Die Flucht in die Sprache*, 30–55.

13 Ball, *Flight Out of Time*, 26.

14 I am referring to the so-called "magic bishop" episode that is described in full in *Flight Out of Time*, 70–71.

15 Ball, *Flight Out of Time*, 68. As in English, the word *Vokabel* refers especially to words, not *Vokale* (or vowels), which suggests that Ball's key fantasy is closely aligned with the Futurist dismantling of the sentence and the boundaries that it imposes upon meaning.

16 In *Flight Out of Time* (54), Ball writes: "Nowhere are the weaknesses of a poem revealed as much as in a public reading. One thing is certain: art is joyful only as long as it has richness and life. Reciting aloud has become the touchstone of the quality of a poem for me, and I have learned (from the stage) to what extent today's literature is worked out as a problem at the desk and is made for the spectacles of the collector instead of for the ears of living human beings."

17 Ball, *Flight Out of Time*, 57.

18 *Tenderenda* 11.7–8.

19 Ball, *Flight Out of Time*, 63. The opening paragraph of the First Dada Manifesto rehearses the same meanings, adding only that in German *dada* can mean "good-bye," "get off my back," or "be seeing you sometime," and in Rumanian "yes, indeed, you are right, that's it. But of course, yes, definitely, right" (*Flight Out of Time*, 220). For an exhaustive analysis of the various legends circulating around the discovery of the label Dada, see John Elderfield, "Dada: The Mystery of the Word," 238–51, in *Flight Out of Time*.

20 Cited from Ball, *Flight Out of Time*, 221. Lilienstein recurs as a journalist in Chapter V of *Tenderenda*.

21 Ball, *Flight Out of Time*, 220–21.

22 Cited from Hammer, "Formative Esotericism in Zurich DADA," 113.

23 Ball confesses as much in the prologue to *Flight Out of Time*: "I went to Berlin in 1910 or 1911. The west seemed to me then to be like an Oriental city, and I

tried to adapt myself as best I could. Since then I have often been taken for a Jew, and I certainly cannot deny that I felt affinities with the Berlin Orient" (*Flight Out of Time*, 5).

24 On this subject, see the catalogue *Monte Verità / Berg der Wahrheit*, ed. Harald Szeemann (Milan: Electa, 1980).

25 The quotation is from the 1933 manifesto "La radia," written by Marinetti and Pino Masnata and anthologized in *Teoria e invenzione futurista*, ed. Luciano de Maria (Verona: Mondadori, 1968), 176–80.

26 Although Evola's work is relatively unknown to the English-speaking public, he became a key philosopher within the Italian fascist fold during the late 1930s; his influence continues to be felt among philo-Nazi neofascist groups. On Evola, see Thomas Sheehan, "Julius Evola and the Metaphysics of Fascism," *Stanford Italian Review* 8:1–2 (1986): 279–92. Two brief excerpts from Evola's writings are available in Jeffrey T. Schnapp, *A Primer of Italian Fascism*, trans. Olivia Sears and Jeffrey T. Schnapp (Lincoln: University of Nebraska Press, 2000), 279–93.

27 The case of Joris Karl Huysmans, also a convert to ultra-Catholicism like Ball and Papini, comes to mind as well.

28 *Tenderenda*, 65. For an excellent concise portrait of Ball's antirationalist stance and intellectual debts, see Anson Rabinbach, *In the Shadow of Catastrophe: German Intellectuals Between Apocalypse and Enlightenment* (Berkeley: University of California Press, 1997), 66–96.

29 Ball, *Flight Out of Time*, 202. The theme of tenderness is further addressed on p. 80, but with respect to grace and graciousness, attributes Ball finds lacking in the German language and the German character.

30 Jacobus de Voragine, *The Golden Legend*, trans. Granger Ryan and Helmut Ripperger (New York: Arno Press, 1969), 437. The tripartite characterization of Lawrence's powers is based upon medical and naturalistic writings on the properties of the laurel, to which was attributed the power to break up kidney stones, to cure deafness, and to ward off lightning.

31 Ibid. 441.

32 Ibid. 442.

33 Cashman Prince has suggested to me that Ball's aversion to entitling his work *Tendenda the Fantast* might have to do with the interference provided by the German word *Tendenz*, which would have cast the titular hero in a "tendentious" rather than austere light.

34 "In the genius, theatricality of intuition is inherent, that multiplicity of reflection that produces ideas. So is sexual changeability, the capacity that enables him to change from the male to the female viewpoint at will. The insights and freedoms that originated here have now been popularized and can be studied everywhere. The hermaphroditic element is, however, only a part of the general protean ability; its foundations go deeper" (Ball, *Flight Out of Time*, 7–8). Prawer interestingly compares Laurentius Tenderenda to Tiresias in T. S. Eliot's *Waste Land*, though without touching upon the common thread of hermaphroditism ("Hugo Ball's *Tenderenda der Phantast*," 221).

35 Ball, *Flight Out of Time*, 29.

36 The only full study to date of Hammer's work on Ball is Joel Lee Coleman's "Rewriting the Game: Dada, Critical Revision and Theories in Play," Ph.D. dissertation, University of Georgia, 1998, 200–208, 241–52.

37 Cited from Hammer's translation of *Tenderenda*, 26.

38 Hammer's image relies in part upon "Hymn 3" in *Tenderenda*, dedicated to the "Chaldean archangel," which contains the verse "You *cymbalum mundi*, coral of the other world, master of fluidity." See *Tenderenda*, 87.

39 On the commonplace of the boy–old man, see Ernst Robert Curtius's classic study *European Literature and the Latin Middle Ages*, trans. Willard Trask, Bollingen Series 36 (Princeton: Princeton University Press, 1973), 98–101.

40 "Ficcaï li occhi per lo cotto aspetto, / sì che 'l viso abbrusciato non difese / la conoscenza süa al mio 'ntelletto" (*Inferno* 15.26–28, cited from *The Divine Comedy of Dante Alighieri*, ed. and trans. Robert M. Durling [New York and Oxford: Oxford University Press, 1996], 230). All subsequent citations and translations are from this edition.

41 The phrase "li mal protesi nervi" (*Inferno* 15.114) applies specifically to Andrea de' Mozzi, bishop of Florence and Vicenza, but more generally to the sin of sodomy.

42 Dante's original reads: "Sieti raccommandato il mio Tesoro, / nel qual io vivo ancora, e più non cheggio" (*Inferno* 15.119).

43 On this subject, one may consult *Les jouets et la tradition moderniste / Toys and the Modernist Tradition* (Montreal: Canadian Center for Architecture, 1993).

44 See Freud, *Three Case Histories: The Wolf Man, The Rat Man, The Psychotic Doctor Schreber*, ed. Philip Rieff (New York: Collier, 1963), 103–86.

45 The label "Blue Tulip" has given rise to various speculations, but the most probable hypothesis is that a veiled allusion is intended to the *Blaue Reiter* group that first assembled in 1911 in Munich around Franz Marc and Wassily Kandinsky. Kandinsky left Germany in 1914, so the fable of Johann's exodus may have some basis both in Ball's own movement from Munich to Berlin and Kandinsky's return to his homeland.

TENDERENDA THE FANTAST

BY HUGO BALL

Illustrated and translated by JONATHAN HAMMER

Annotated by Jeffrey T. Schnapp

O vous, messeigneurs et mes dames,
Qui contemplez ceste painture,
Plaise vous prier pour les âmes
De ceulx qui sont en sepulture.[1]

—Saint Bernard

I THE RISE OF THE SEER[2]

One is transported into the excitement of an imaginary city. A new god is expected. Donnerkopf[3] (who will not be mentioned again in this novel) has changed his place of residence, now living in a tower from which he issues forth colorful[4] bulletins that are meant to inform the unfolding of events. The tepid evening falls. A charlatan appears in the marketplace suggesting a possible ascension to heaven. Toward this purpose he has dreamt up his own theory, which he expounds far and wide. This idea, however, runs aground because of public skepticism. What are the consequences to be.

1 Oh you, ladies and gentlemen / who contemplate this painting / let it please you to pray for the souls / of those buried within" (editor's translation). This epigraph was extracted by Ball from *Le Latin mystique: Les poètes de l'Antiphonaire et la symbolique au moyen âge*, ed. Rémy de Gourmont (Paris: Mercure de France, 1892), a favorite book of Ball in later years.
2 First performed on the stage of the Cabaret Voltaire on February 7, 1916.
3 Literally translated, Donnerkopf means "thunderhead."
4 In one of the typescript versions of *Tenderenda*, the phrase is *hieroglyphische Bulletins*, or "hieroglyphic bulletins."

On this day Donnerkopf was prevented from attending the festivities. Behold, he sat before charts and circles, proclaiming the wisdom of the stratosphere. He unwound from the tower long scrolls of papyrus painted with signs and animals; through these he warned the people who stood below the perches of the screeching host of angels angrily circling the tower. On this day, though, someone carried a banner on a long pole through the city, upon which was written:

Talita kumi,[5] arise young maiden;
You are the one, the chosen one.
Gutter daughter, mother of joy,
Those hung and those banished
invoke your being.
Free us, bless us,
Unknown one,
Step forward!

Through fasting and purgation the city prepared for the advent of a new God. There were already some in the crowd who claimed to have met him in the throng. A warning was issued stating that anyone caught visiting or entering the belfries or rag towers without permission would suffer living death. The causal nexus was blown up afresh and exposed, clear to all, as food to the holy spiders. Hand-wringing scholars and artists with rattles and bagpipes moved along in an imploring coffee procession. Hanging water signs and siphons of glass emerged from all the draughts and sky hatches. There, crossing the marketplace as if by some calling, walked the violet-faced seer[6] commanding the laughing houses, the stars, the moon, and the crowd, saying:

"The sky stands in lemon yellow. In lemon yellow stand the fields of the soul. We have cocked our heads to the earth and opened wide our ears. We have spread out our baldrics and tabards and the back of clacking porcelain blinks in the structure.

"Verily I say unto you: my humility concerns not you, but GOD. All search for a happiness of which they are not deserving. No one has as many enemies as they could. Man is chimera, a wonder, a Godly approximate, filled with scheming forethought and deceit.

"One day, because of my own curiosity and suspicion, I no longer knew

5 *Talita kumi* is but the first of many nonsense invocations and magic formulas found in *Tenderenda.*
6 On the violet-faced seer as interpreted by Hammer, see p. 12 of the introduction.

myself. Behold, I turned about and withdrew unto myself. Behold, the candle burned and dripped upon my head. My first impression, however, was both great and small, that is paradox. Great and small, that is relativism. Behold, my finger shot out, burnt upon contact with the sun. Behold, the hands of the clock tower then split open the surface of the street. You trust you are feeling, but you are being felt."

Pausing to scratch his ear, he cast a glance to the fifth floor of the fourth building. There, Lunette's leg, clad in rose-colored silk, stuck out from the window.[7] Upon the leg perched two winged creatures sucking blood.

And the seer continued:

"Verily no thing is as it seems. It is possessed by living spirits, imps silenced for as long as one gazes; when the mask is removed it transforms, becoming monstrous. For years I bore the weight of things desiring freedom. Whereupon I recognized their dimensions. My fervor was heightened. Terrible life! My arms spread as in defense. I took flight, flying as an arrow above the rooftops."

Now one could see that the seer, drunk from the effervescence of his own words, had spoken unbreakable promises. Flapping loudly with both hands, he lifted himself up and, as a demonstration, flew a short stretch into the evening, inclined into a curve, and came to an effortless stop after a few hopping steps.

The mob, hanging hip deep out of windows everywhere around the marketplace, was startled. The rabble shook their heads in displeasure and disbelief, waving the salt trumpets and paper lanterns they had brought along with might and main, and shouting: "The magnifying glass! The magnifying glass!"

For it was common knowledge that the seer often used such a glass on his rounds. Thus all were certain that the tricks performed by the seer were nothing but a swindle involving this instrument. There was also an interlude during which time a busybody woman who had been waving on a flagpole was torn away by the evening wind and driven eastward over the roofs. Item: a cock with a ruffled sickle flew high above the ladies' fans, which stood as a sign of divisive vanity.

The seer, embarrassed and disheartened, did indeed produce the magnifying glass. The glass was about the size of a Russian swing, like the kind seen at fairs.[8] The glass was extraordinarily well polished, framed in silver, and fastened gracefully to a long wooden pole. Holding the mirror aloft in a tragic pose,

7 *Lunette*, of course, means "little moon" if interpreted in Latinate fashion, with extended meanings including half-moon-shaped windows.
8 As indicated in the text, the Russian swing was a fairground entertainment.

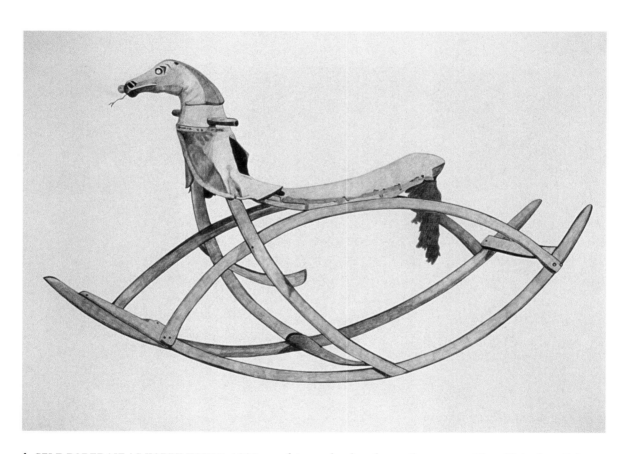

1 SELF-PORTRAIT AS HOBBY-HORSE, 1995, graphite and colored pencil on paper, 22 × 30 inches. Private collection, Columbus, Ohio.

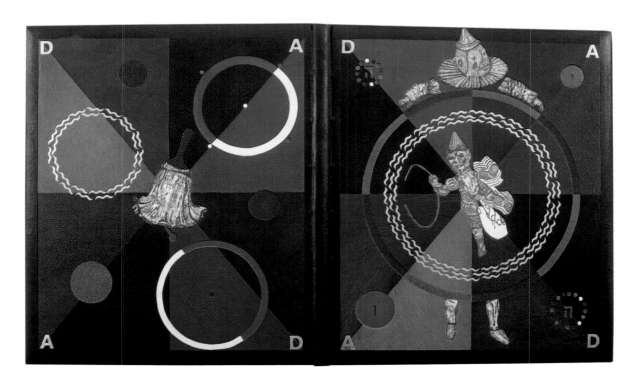

2 THREE RINGS FOR HILDEGARD, 1997, unique book cover, mixed media, 19 × 31 inches. Private collection, Hamburg, Germany.

he suddenly rose up and shattered the mirror, the fragments splintered, and he vanished into the yellow sea of the evening.

Yet the glass splinters of the marvelous broken mirror cut the houses, the people, the cattle, the tightrope acts, the mine shafts, and all nonbelievers, so the number of those cut increased from day to day.

II JOHANN THE CAROUSEL HORSE[9]

In the summer of 1914, a visionary community of poets smell mischief and
resolve to bring their symbolic hobbyhorse[10] to safety in time. How Johann first
objects and then agrees. The wanderings and obstacles encountered under the
leadership of a certain Benjamin. In distant regions one meets the chieftain
Feuerschein,[11] who turns out to be a police informer. Followed by historiological
comments concerning a Berlin police bitch in labor.

9   First performed during an evening dedicated to German authors held at the Zunfthaus zur
    Zimmerleuten in Zurich on December 17, 1915.
10 One typescript reads *Stecken- und Lieblingspferd,* which could be roughly translated as
    "hobby and sweetheart horse," the addition of *Liebling* emphasizing the affective, even
    erotic ties foregrounded in Hammer's reading.
11 The name Feuerschein means "fire glow" in German. In *Flametti,* Feuerschein appears as
    a fire-eating vaudeville impresario.

"One thing is certain," said Benjamin, "intelligence is dilettantism. Intelligence no longer fools us. They look inward, we look outward. They are Jesuits of practicality. An intellect like Savonarola[12] does not exist. Intelligent like Manasseh,[13] yes. Their bible is the civil code of law."

"You're right," said Jopp,[14] "intelligence is suspicious: it's the quick wit of fading advertising executives. The ascetic's club The Ugly Thigh is the discoverer of the Platonic idea. Today the 'thing in itself' is mere shoe polish. The world is sassy and packed with epilepsy."

"Enough," said Benjamin,[15] "it makes me sick when I hear of 'law,' 'contrast,' 'also,' and 'therefore.' Why should a zebu be a hummingbird? I hate additions and perfidy. One should let be a seagull who prunes her feathers in the sun, and not say to her 'therefore,' she suffers from that."

"Therefore," said Stiselhäher,[16] "let's carry the hobbyhorse to safety and sing a hymn to the fabulous."

"I don't know," said Benjamin, "we ought rather to first carry the horse to safety. There are indications that something bad is yet to come."

And indeed there were indications that something bad was yet to come. A head had been found uninterruptedly yelling "Blood! Blood!" and the flexing muscles no longer functioned. In the banking houses they were discrediting the "watch on the Rhine."

"All right then," said Stiselhäher again, "let's carry Johann the hobbyhorse to safety. One never knows what may happen."

On a sky-blue bar floor, wide-eyed, stood Johann the hobbyhorse bathed in sweat.

"No, no," said Johann. "I was born here and I shall die here." This, how-

12 A reference, naturally, to the fifteenth-century Dominican preacher Girolamo Savonarola (1452–98), remembered for his apocalyptic sermons preached in the public squares of Florence. Savonarola is another Saint Lawrence figure inasmuch as he was tortured on the rack, hanged, and burned on a pyre.

13 Manasseh, the son of Hezekiah, appears in 2 Kings 21 as a Jewish king who established a syncretistic national religion in Judah, encompassing elements from Assyrian astral religion and the worship of idols such as Baal.

14 The name derives from the word *Joppe* (f.), which signifies "heavy jacket."

15 The name Benjamin, of course, has broad biblical resonances, being associated with one of Jacob's sons (the object of several contemplative treatises by Richard of Saint Victor), as well as with the tribe of the Benjaminites. Green suggests that Ball's Benjamin may recall the title character of Carl Eisenstein's *Bebuquin oder die Dilettanten des Wunders* (Bebuquin, or the Dilettantes of Wonder) (Berlin: Verlag der Wochenshcrift Dei Aktion, 1912), given the well-established impact of this work on *Tenderenda*.

16 Like most of Ball's names, *Stiselhäher* is meant as comic. *Stisel* is probably derived from *Stiesel*, meaning a "churlish person"; *Häher* signifies "jay."

ever, was not quite true. Johann's mother came from Denmark and his father was Hungarian. At last they all agreed and that night they fled.

"Parbleu," said Stiselhäher. "Here the world has come to an end. Here there is a wall. We can go no further." Indeed, there was a wall. Ascending toward the sky.

"Ridiculous," said Jopp, "we've lost touch. We went into the night forgetting to hang bail stones for ourselves. No wonder we're floating in air."

"Nonsense," said Stiselhäher, "there's something fishy here. I refuse to go farther. There are fish heads strewn about. There were sea monsters at work here. There were sea cows being milked here."

"The devil only knows," said Runzelmann,[17] "I feel spooky about the whole thing. They're pulling the charlatan's shirt over our ears too." He shuddered violently.

"Halt everything!" ordered Benjamin. "What's over there? A paddy wagon? Green with barred windows? What's growing there? Agaves, palm fans and tamarinds? Jopp, look up what that means in the book of signs."

"Grave matter," said Stiselhäher, "a paddy wagon among agaves. Already that's suspicious. God only knows where we're stuck."

"Poppycock," shouted Benjamin, "if it weren't dark we could see exactly what was going on. That quack of a horse doctor has led us astray."

"The fact is," said Jopp, "we're in front of a wall. We can't go on from here. Gundelfleck,[18] light the lantern." Gundelfleck roamed about in his pocket, but could only produce a powerful light-blue organ pipe. At least he carried this with him.

"Come closer, gentlemen," a voice was suddenly heard; "you're barking up the wrong tree." It was Chieftain Feuerschein. "Where are you going, groping in the night and parading about awake? Take off your celluloid noses! Unmask yourselves! We know who you are! What kind of instruments are you carrying there?"

"There are rods and bell sticks and fool's whips, with your permission."

"What kind of instrument is that?"

"That is a Nuremberg funnel."

"And what's that ball of cotton there on the leash?"

"Oh, that's Johann the hobbyhorse packed carefully in cotton."

17 Runzelmann is another humorous name that, literally translated, means "wrinkle man."
18 *Gundelfleck* is best translated as "ivy patch."

3 BUTCHER CLOWN, 1995, graphite and colored pencil on paper, 22 × 30 inches. Private collection, Columbus, Ohio.

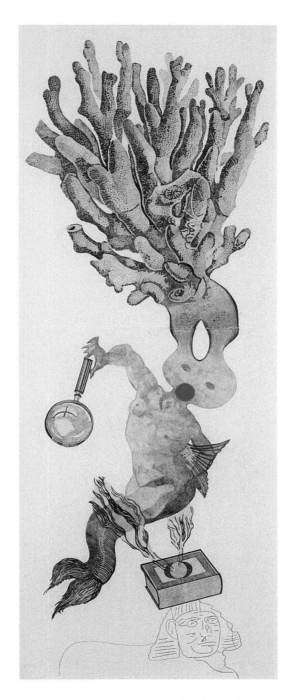

4 THE VIOLET-FACED SEER, 1995, graphite
and colored pencil on paper, 82 × 34 inches.
Collection of the San Francisco Museum of
Modern Art, Ruth Nash Fund purchase.

"Fiddlesticks, what are you doing with a hobbyhorse here in the Libyan desert? Where did you get the horse from?"

"It is, as it were, our symbol, Mr. Feuerschein. With your permission. You see in us the sterilized visionary club of the 'Blue Tulip.'"[19]

"Symbol here, symbol there. You kept the horse from performing his military duty. What is your name?"

"What a terrible guy!" said Jopp. "This is pure Robinsonism."[20]

"Pooh," said Stiselhäher, "he's a fiction. It's all been caused by this Benjamin. He dreams this all up, and we're the ones who have to suffer . . ."

"My dear Mr. Feuerschein! Your confederated manliness and your political complexion do not impress us. Nor your borrowed movie dramatics! But just a word for your enlightenment: we are visionaries. We no longer believe in intellectualism. We have taken to the road in order to save this animal, to whom we are completely devoted, from the mob."

"I can understand you," said Feuerschein, "but I am unable to help. Step into the paddy wagon. The horse too. Forward march, no objections. Get in!"

The bitch Rosalie was in heavy labor. Five young police dogs saw the light of the world. At the same time a Chinese sea monster was caught in the Berlin Spree canal. The animal was brought to the police station.

JOHANN THE CAROUSEL HORSE

19 The label "Blue Tulip" may evoke the Blue Rider group of artists, though Meyer and
      Schütte note a critical review by Ball of a production of Paul Claudel's play *Annunciation*,
      published in *Revolution* on November 15, 1913, in which he refers to the *Dilettanten-
      verein blau Tulpe* (the Blue Tulip Dilettante Association).
20 Robinsonism alludes to Robinson Crusoe.

36

III THE DECLINE OF THE DANCE MAKER[21]

As the name implies, a dance maker is one who makes dances and loves sensations. He is one of those desperate types without spiritual fortitude, affected by the slightest impression. Hence, his tragic end. The poet has placed it here for special emphasis. We will see how the dance maker succumbs bit by bit to obsession, then to deep apathy, until finally, after fruitless attempts to procure his own alibi, he sinks into that religiously tainted paralysis which, when coupled with excess, seals his complete physical and moral ruin.

Then Machetanz[22] suddenly felt his temples throb. The productive streams that had warmed and enveloped his body died out and hung away like long saffron

21 First performed on the stage of the Cabaret Voltaire on March 26, 1916.
22 *Machetanz* literally means "dance maker."

wallpapers. A wind had bent back his hands and feet. His spine, a squeaking pulley, spiraled skyward.

Rancorous, Machetanz grabbed a stone that cried kitty-corner-like out of a building and began blindly defending himself. A ripping squall of blue thugs demolished him. A sky collapsed brightly. An air shaft tipped diagonally; across the sky there flew a chain of winged pregnant women.

The gas works, the brewery, and the domes of the city halls began to shake and drone amid the honking of the drums. Demons with multicolored feathers tugged, plucked at, and bashed into his brains. Across the marketplace, sinking into the stars, there loomed the sickle of a greenish ship's hull propped up on its tip, perpendicular.

Machetanz drove his two index fingers into his ears, scraping out the last shabby remnants of sun that had taken refuge there. Apocalyptic glitter broke out. The blue thugs blew into conch trumpets. They climbed up balustrades of light, descending into a glittery state.

Machetanz was overcome with nausea. He was choking on the wrong god. He ran with uplifted arms, stumbled, and fell on his face. A voice cried out behind. He closed his eyes, feeling himself propelled over the town in three mighty leaps. Siphons sipped at the strength of the mystic container.

Machetanz fell to his knees, prostrate in his withered priestly vestments, and bared his teeth toward heaven. The house fronts are grave rows heaped one on the other. Cities of copper at the edge of the moon. Casemates that waver at night on the tail of a shooting star. A poster culture peels away, torn to pieces. Machetanz raves, seized by Saint Vitus's dance. One, two, one, two, ways to kill the flesh. "Pan-Catholicism" he bellowed in his blindness. He established a general consulate for public protest, being the first to lodge a complaint. He expounded on the compelling phenomenon of his excesses and wake-dream mania in a cinedramatic manner. He was flung about in a magnetic bottle. He burns in the pipes of a subterranean sewage system. A beautiful scar adorns Machetanz's eye, which glows with a white shimmer.

In a zigzag-patterned shirt, he balances on a high tower of ether. He rents the great Ferris sweep and, rising, comes bursting through the spokes of the imagined huge wheel. He is threatened by the faces of quick decisions, of the agile skin of the head, by bleating skepticism. With broken lung wings he hops out of a goblin's hand.

Friends leave him. "Machetanz, Machetanz!" he crows down from the chimney. He escapes the nexus. He rises, a segment of the solar eclipse, above the crooked domes and towers of the drunken cities. Sleepless and bedded down in a baby carriage, he is dragged across the street. He is overshadowed by the landscape of blushing, of grief, of marital bliss.

Machetanz mumbles himself in decadence. He deposits all-encompassing anxiety complexes. He fabricates lukewarm inhibitions, counterfeit coins of spiritual cataracts and sensations. At night he coils up in the body of a whore. The skin of fear creeps up behind his ears. "Do you think, you fools," and he smacks the ground, the foam at his mouth a blue cloud. He crawls out to the sun. He wants the experience. The grass is growing enviously and drives him back into darkness. Curtains billow and a house disappears. The catalepsy of destruction. Tongues project sharply and incline toward the pavement in a red rain of arrows.

Gagny, the tin one, combs his part in order to think. Dagny, the fish's bride, nurses him. Shimmering on her right side, Musikon.[23] Machetanz has killed a captain with a songbook. He has invented an artificial swimming island. He dabbles in prayer processions and feels devotion to the vagabond Jesus. He holds up the lantern at the death registry and when he lets out water it is vinegarish clay.

But there is no relief. He cannot bear these turbulences, detonations, and radium fields. "Quantity is everything" he shouts. "Syphilis is a serious venereal disease." He takes an acid bath to rid himself of his plumed body. What remains: a corn, a pair of golden glasses, false teeth, and an amulet. And the soul: an ellipsis.

Machetanz smiles bitterly: "originality is a catarrh of the windpipe. Painful and incredible. To commit murder. A murder is something that cannot be denied. Never and ever. To keep things running smoothly. To always love the poor. To have God as a supplement. This is firm ground." And he blew Musikon into the nape of her neck. Whereupon she evaporated.

And he wrote his testament. With ink made of urine. He had none other. For he sat in jail. And there he cursed: the visionary, Dagny, Johann the hobbyhorse, his poor mother, and many other people. Then he died. A palm forest grew in a soup made of soda. A horse moved its legs forward. A mourning flag waved over a hospital.

23 There is no known referent for Gagny, but as noted by Green, Dagny was the name of the
    wife of the decadent Berlin poet Stanislav Prybyszewski (1868–1927), which suggests a
    broader identification between the neurasthenic Machetanz and Prybyszewski. Musikon
    is a Hellenism, meaning "music."

5 LANDSCAPE FROM THE UPPER INFERNO, 1997, graphite and colored pencil on paper, 39 × 25 inches. Private collection, Lanzarote, Spain.

6 JUMPING JACK WITH HIS NOSE IN HIS HAND, 1996, graphite and colored pencil on paper, 30 × 22 inches. Private collection, Zurich, Switzerland.

Landscape from the upper inferno.[24] A concert of great cacophonous noises that astonish even the animals. The animals appear, some as musicians caterwauling, some in the embalmed state of a diorama. The aunties from the seventh dimension participate obscenely in the witches' Sabbath.

> The red skies, mimulli mamei,[25]
> In the midst of stomach cramps lie.
> The red skies fall into the sea,
> Mimulli mamei, a pain in the belly.
>
> The blue cats, fofolli mamei,
> Scratch on the rust-cragged corrugated tin.

24 Dante separated Hell into two sections: the Upper Inferno, consisting in circles one through seven, and the Lower Inferno, circles eight and nine.
25 *Mimulli mamei* is another nonsense formula, chosen for its euphony and rhythm.

O lalalo lalalo lalala!
There is also a purring auntie nearby.

The purring auntie lifts up out of the snow
In the air its trilling trousers skirts clothes.
O lalalo lalalo lalalo!
Then said the faun: "It matters little or no."

The clay pigeon falls from the roof.
The doubled Johann springs for it up on his hoofs.
O lalalo and mimulli mamei!
Two scratching its iron make the violin cry.

The horse and the ass looked askance
At the snow goose who called from a distance
The blue tuba gives way—
Then the multiplication tables they say.

O lalalo lalalo lalalo,
The head made of glass and the hands of a scarecrow.
O lalalo lalalo lalalo!
Cinnabar, cries of murder and woe!

7 GOAT PUSHING CLOWN, 1995, graphite and colored pencil on paper, 20 × 25 inches. Private collection, San Francisco.

8 JOHANN THE HOBBYHORSE, 1995, graphite and colored pencil on paper, 30 × 33 inches. Private collection, Columbus, Ohio.

A mystical occurrence that takes place in the blackest of inkish Hell. Tenderenda recounts a tale to a rally of ghosts and deceased ones included with Satanopolean initiates and habitués.[27] He assumes there is a general knowledge of the names and places, a familiarity with subterranean institutions.

A journalist had escaped. A gray figure, he overshadowed the grazing fields of Satanopolis. They decided to launch an attack against him. The revolutionary tribunal gathered. They launched an attack against the gray figure, who moved about on the grazing fields of Satanopolis. It is here they found his house at $26\frac{1}{2}$ Mount, where stands the cauldron of trinity. They surrounded the house

---

26 Naturally, Satanopolis is the city of Satan, in keeping with the infernal characterization of many of *Tenderenda*'s landscapes and places.

27 On the name *Tenderenda*, see pp. 8–9 of the introduction to this volume.

with stick lanterns. Their moon horns shown pale yellow in the night. They all ran up with birdcages in hand.

"That's a very pretty rabbit flusher you've got there," said Mr. Schmidt to Mr. Schultz.

"Spinozan affront!" Mr. Meyer said to Mr. Schmidt. Then he mounted his nag, which was his weakness, and rode away annoyed.

In the meantime, many knitting guillotine furies by the side, it was decided that the journalist should be taken by storm. The house that he held was known as the moon house. He had barricaded it with mattresses made of ether waves and placed the cauldron on the roof, so that he stood uniquely under the protection of the heavens. He nourished himself on calamus roots, yogurt, and candy. He also placed about him the dead bodies that rained down abundantly through the chimney from the earth above. This way he could hold out comfortably for a few weeks. So he did not worry much. He felt fine and to kill time he studied the twenty-seven different ways of sitting and spooking. His name was Lilienstein.[28]

A meeting took place in the City Hall of the Devil. The Devil appeared with Ridicule and anyone who's anyone in Paris. He said something incomprehensible and sang *Rigoletto.* They yelled up, calling him a strutting simpleton, and told him to quit his jokes. And they deliberated whether to burn down the house Lilienstein held by means of his pince-nez, with dance, or to have it devoured by bedbugs and fleas.

The Devil on the balcony was seized by an urge to swing his legs and said: "The lower parts of Marat end in a dagger.[29] He has mattresses made of ether waves in front of his house, and towers of flies hover around him in the bluish color of their foundations. He has rubbed the fat of dead corpses all over and made himself insensible. Try to go over there with hordes of people, each with a drum on his belt. Perhaps . . . it may succeed." The wife of the Devil was a svelte, blue-eyed blonde. She sat on a female ass and kept at his side.

And so they turned around, marched back, and sang to the beat of the drum. And they returned to the moon house and saw the ether-wave mattresses and Lilienstein in full light as he strolled. And the smoke of his lunch escaped from the chimney.

And he pasted up a great poster that read:

28 As noted in the introduction, the name Lilienstein is best translated as "stone lilies." The name was cited in the First Dada Manifesto.
29 A reference, presumably, to the French revolutionist Jean-Paul Marat (1743–93), founder of the journal *L'Ami du Peuple* and leader of the extremist Cordelier faction.

Qui hic mixerit aut cacarit

Habeat deos inferos et superos iratos."

[Whoever here pisses or shits

angers the gods of both heaven and hell.]

(He had not thought this up himself; it came from Luther.) And a second poster which read:

"Whoever is afraid, should put on armor.

If it helps, it helps.

For Scheblimini[30] lives and remains alive.

Sedet ad dexteris meis [He sits by my right side].

The sore spot."

I can tell you, they were gnawing with anger. And now they did not know how they would flush out Lilienstein. But then a thought occurred to them: they threw dogweed and honey over Lilienstein's house. Then he was forced to come out. And they pursued him.

Fleeing, he stumbled over the sleeping cars that stood in the street on account of the sleeping sickness. Fleeing, he tripped over the legs of Petroleum who sat at the corner rubbing his belly. Fleeing over the shacks of the patroness of the toilets who, spitting children, made seventy-two stars of goodness and thirty-six stars of evil dance on long strings. And they pursued him.

An apoplexy wallops in sky-blue ribbons. Blue thirsty snails crawl. Whoever has seen this phallus knows all the others. He runs past the octopus who studies Greek grammar and rides a bicycle. He passes lamp-lit towers and high blast furnaces where dead soldiers' corpses burn through the night. And he escaped.

In taverns of the Devil a manifesto was read. A 6,000-franc reward was offered to whomever could inform or locate a reliable source regarding his whereabouts in Satanopolis or find the tracks of this monster, the journalist Lilienstein. It was read to the sound of a chorus of trombones. But in vain.

They had already forgotten him, and each had gone his own way when he was discovered on the Italian Corso. People were promenading on sky-blue horses, and as it was hot, the ladies carried long-handled parasols.

They noticed him on the parasol of a lady. He had built himself a nest there and, in so doing, was found, fit for hatching. He bared his teeth and screeched

30 *Scheblimini* is another comic name, combining German and Latin elements. A *Scheibe* is a "disk" or "slice"; *limini* echoes the Latin *limen*, or "threshold."

in a piercing tone: "Zirrizittig-Zirritig."[31] But to no avail. The lady on whose parasol he was strolling, was tugged back and forth. They cursed, spat on, and accused her. She was given a kick in the rear, for they thought she was a spy. Then he fell out of the nest along with the eggs, and cries rose up.

But they only tore away his paper suit. He himself escaped, withdrawing to the rafters of the railway station, way up where the smoke lingers. It was clear that he could not stay there for very long.

Indeed, he came down five days later and was brought before the judge. He looked pitiful. His face was darkened by coal dust, his hands soiled by inky black filth. He carried a revolver in his trouser pocket. In his breast pocket, next to his billfold, the *Handbook of Criminal Psychology*, by Ludwig Rubiner.[32] He continued to bare his teeth "Zirritig-Zirrizitig." Then the octopi came out of their holes and laughed. Then the Zackopadores[33] came out and sniffed him. About his head flitted magic dragons and seahorses.

And they put him on trial: "To have ruined, in his grey form, the grazing land of the mystics. To have attracted attention through all sorts of mischief." But the Devil became his advocate and defended him. "Anal sputter and indolence," said the Devil "what do you want from him? Behold, here stands a man. Do you want me to wash my hands of innocence or should he be tortured?" And the poor and the beggars pressed close roaring: "Lord, help us, we are feverish." But he pushed them back with the flat of his hand and said: "Please, later." And the trial was postponed.

The next day, however, there returned a great crowd with straight razors screaming: "Hand him over. He has blasphemed against God and Devil. He is a journalist. He has soiled our moon house, and built a nest on the parasol of a lady."

And the Devil said to Lilienstein: "Defend yourself." And a gentleman from the public shouted loudly: "This gentleman has no common ground with *The Action*."[34]

31 *Zirrizittig* is a nonsense name, though it is spun out of the adjective *zitterig*, which means "shaky" or "quaky."
32 Green as well as Meyer and Schütt all note that Rubiner, a politically engaged Expressionist poet and acquaintance of Ball, was the author of *Kriminalsonette* (Criminal Sonnets), written in collaboration with Friedrich Eisenlohr and Livingstone Hahn (published as *Kriminalsonette*, ed. Rudolph Braun and Gunther Schulz [Stuttgart: Scherz, 1962]). Also worth mentioning is that "Dada Mr. Rubiner" is cited in the First Dada Manifesto, right before "Dada Mr. Anastasius Lilienstein."
33 The German nonsense word *Zackopadoren*, though untranslatable, may be derived from *Zacke*, or "sharp point."
34 As noted by Green, Ball had once collaborated with this Expressionist review but in 1915 broke with its stance in favor of the Russian Revolution, leading the then editor,

9 THE IMAGINARY CITY, 1997, graphite and colored pencil on paper, 36 × 60 inches. Collection of the artist, courtesy of Matthew Marks Gallery, New York.

10 THE JUBILANT ASS, 1997, graphite and colored pencil on paper, 39 × 25 inches.
Collection of the artist, courtesy of Matthew Marks Gallery, New York.

And Lilienstein fell to his knees, imploring the stars, the moon, the crowd, shouting loudly: "Autolax is the best. Made of soft pulp and funnel-like cones tied to fibrous rope, antiquity already knew this. The Soxlet apparatus is a contemporary invention. The best laxative is Autolax.[35] It consists of plant extracts. Listen to me: of plant extracts! It need not be mentioned that it is a product of German industry," he mumbled in desperation. "Take this recipe. I implore you. In exchange let me go. What have I done, that you persecute me so? Behold, I am the king of the Jews."

Then they broke into uncontrollable laughter and the Devil said: "The gall, the gall, would you believe that." And a man from the crowd bellowed: "Crucify him, crucify him!"

And he was sentenced to eat nothing but his own self-made shit. And the Devil painter Meideles painted his portrait before he was handed over to the executioner. And all flags were dripping with scorn and lye.

Franz Pfemfert, to declare, "Die Aktion hat mit dem Schriftsteller Hugo Ball nichts zu tun." (*The Action* has nothing to do with the writer Hugo Ball), cited from Meyer and Schütt, *Tenderenda*, 111.

35 Autolax was apparently an actual brand of laxative. Green mentions that the "soxlet apparatus" was invented by Franz Soxhleth (1848–1926) for purposes of chemical extraction.

VI THE GRAND HOTEL METAPHYSICS[36]

The birth of Dadaism. Mulche-Mulche,[37] the quintessence of fantasy, gives birth to the young Mr. Foetus, high up in those reaches that, surrounded by Music, Dance, Stupidity, and Godly Familiarity, are clearly distinguished from their opposites.

They were less upset by the speeches of Messrs. Clemenceau and Lloyd George, by Ludendorff's gunfire,[38] than by the uncertain group of Dadaist wandering prophets who proclaimed childishness in their own way.

36 First performed at the Dada Gallery in Zurich on April 28, 1917.
37 According to Rechner-Zimmermann, *Mulche-Mulche* refers to milk for the production of cheese in Alemanic ("den sprechenden Namen *Mulche-Mulche* . . . aus dem Alemannischen kommt und 'Milch zur Bereitung von Käse' oder 'Molke' bedeutet" [*Die Flucht in die Sprache*, 115]).
38 The list includes three prominent leaders of, respectively, France, England, and Germany in World War I. Whereas the first two occupied the position of prime minister, Erich Ludendorff was a general, hence the reference to "gunfire."

In an elevator made of tulips and hyacinths, Mulche-Mulche took herself to the mezzanine of the Grand Hotel Metaphysics. Up there waiting for her were: the Master of Ceremonies, who had to keep the astronomical instruments in order, the Jubilant Ass, who eagerly quenched his thirst in a bucket of raspberry juice, and Musikon, our dear lady made of passacaglie[39] and fugues.

The slender legs of Mulche-Mulche were entirely wrapped in chrysanthemums, so her gait was restricted to very sparing steps. The rose-petaled tongue protruded slightly over her teeth. Golden dew hung from her eyes, and the black blanket of the sky bed, which stood ready, was painted with silver dogs.

The hotel was porous and built out of rubber. Eaves and corners protruded from the upper floor. When Mulche-Mulche disrobed and the shimmer of her eyes colored the sky: yea, the Jubilant Ass had drunk his fill. Yea, he roared a welcome with a far-reaching voice. The Master of Ceremonies bowed in all directions pushing a spyglass near to the banister in order to study celestography.[40] But dancing continuously, a golden flame about the sky bed, Musikon suddenly raised her arms and, behold, the town was cast over with violin shadows.

Mulche-Mulche's eyes consumed themselves in flame. Her body was filled with grain, incense, and myrrh, so the blankets of her bed rose and billowed. The freight of her body was bloated by all kinds of seed and fruit, till the binds burst at the point wherein she was bound.

And there the entire rachitic populace of the area came along in order to obstruct the birth, which threatened the barren land with fertility.

P. T. Bridet,[41] a death flower in his hat, grew on his wooden leg with a shout. A puddle of poison showed up on his cheek. He grimly rushed up from the room of the deceased to angrily meet the incredible.

And there was Pimperling[42] with his screw-on head. His eardrums hung out crumpled from both sides. He wore a sweatband of Northern Lights, the latest style. The type of mass grave digger covered with mire who, powdered over with vanilla, jealous due to his horrid stink, is intent on saving his honor.

39 The *passacaglia* (pl. *passacaglie*) was a dance of Spanish origin, popular in Italy in the seventeenth century. Originally performed in the streets, its name derives from *pasa calle*, or "cross the street."
40 *Cölestographie* in the original: another Ball neologism.
41 Green was the first to note that the name P. T. Bridet may refer to the agronomist Jacques Pierre Bridet, famous for advocating the transformation of human waste into fertilizer. He argues, however, for the identification of Bridet with Gottfried Benn (*Blago Bung*, 166).
42 The name Pimperling echoes the adjective *pimpelig* (or more commonly, *pimplig*), meaning "effeminate." Green proposes an identification with Theodor Däubler, author of the epic *Northern Lights* (*Blago Bung*, 166).

And there was Toto,[43] who had this name and nothing else. His oiled Adam's apple purred against the running wind. He had his Jericho girdle[44] fastened around his belly, so that the quivering rags of his guts would not get lost. Marseillaise, his shibboleth, beamed in red from his chest.

And they besieged the garden, posted guards, and shot at the mezzanine with movie cannons. And this thundered on for days and nights. As a trial balloon, they raised the violet-ray-emitting "Potato Soul." Its light rocket was inscribed "God save the King" or "We come to praise." Through a megaphone they called up to the mezzanine: "The fear of the present devours us." Meanwhile, up there, the busy finger of the Godhead was trying in vain to coax young Mr. Foetus out of Mulche-Mulche's rumbling body. He had reached the point where he cautiously peeked from the gaping mother gate. But with the sly face of a fox he withdrew blinking when he saw the four, Jopp, Musikon, the Godhead, and the Jubilant Ass, with butterfly nets, sticks and poles, and a wet washrag, all united to receive him. And a magisterial sweat broke out of Mulche's reddened body with shots and rays, so that the entire surroundings were flooded by it.

Whereupon those down below were confounded because of their rusted movie artillery and knew not what to do, whether to withdraw or remain. And they asked the advice of the "Potato Soul" and decided to take the lovely spectacle of the Grand Hotel Metaphysics by storm.

As the first of the catapults they brought up the Fashion Idol. This was a shining pinhead with a low forehead loaded up with rhinestones and oriental junk. Because it is lathed from head to foot out of wooden lies and wears an iron heart as a locket on its breast, it may be called the humorless idol.

It towers with a neck all black adorned with bells and the tuning fork of vice high in its right hand. Painted over and over with signs of the Kabala and Talmud, it peers good naturedly out of childish pupils. With six hundred nimble arms it distorts facts and history. At the farthest vertebrae is attached a tin box with an oxyhydrogen blowpipe. And as the oil-anointed dispersion takes place, there drop from its hindquarters generals and gang leaders, inhuman and with their faces dragging in slime.

---

43 The name *Toto* is meant humorously inasmuch as the Latin root means "total" or "all," whereas this particular Toto has nothing but his name. Green convincingly identifies him with Albert Ehrenstein, author of the novel *Tubutsch,* which ends on precisely this phrase (*Blago Bung,* 166).

44 *Jerichobinde* was the name of a Zurich bar mentioned in *Flametti.*

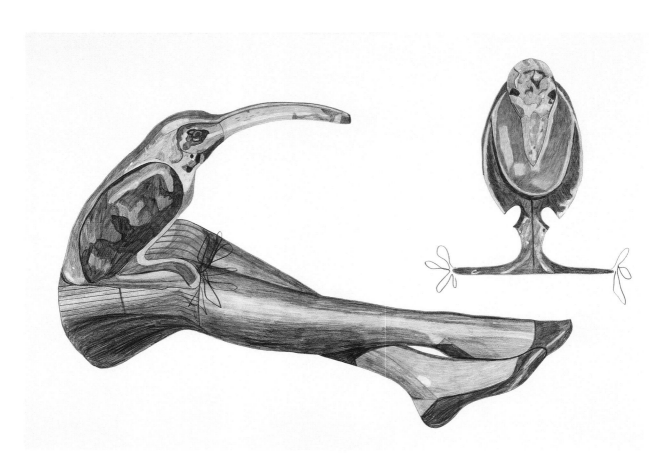

11 LUNETZ'S LEG CLAD IN ROSE-COLORED SILK, 1998, graphite, colored pencil, and watercolor on paper, 46 × 34 inches. Private collection, Beverly Hills.

12 THE CHIEFTAIN FEUERSCHEIN, 1997, watercolor and graphite on paper, 46 × 34 inches. Private collection, Columbus, Ohio.

But from up top, with Musikon's help, Jopp embeds a detonation wire deep into the idol's stomach, packed with hesper, sulfur, aconite, and sulfuric acid.[45] They explode it and the conspiracy is foiled.

As a second idol they bring out the Bearded Dog, so as to rinse with primordial roars and froth the tender anecdote from the mezzanine of the Grand Hotel Metaphysics. With a crowbar the plaster of religions is lifted, so a road and rail are cleared. The "ideological superstructure" stocks fall rapidly. "Oh, crash into bestiality!" complains Bridet. "The magic printing shops of the Holy Ghost no longer suffice to stem the decline."

And there he comes growling and spitting, harnessed to a church running on ball bearings from behind whose curtains fearful priests, prelates, deacons, and *summi episcopi* [archbishops] look out. Vertebrae with five spines uphold his mangy coat into which troops have been tattooed. His fleeting forehead enthrones a reproduction of Golgotha. Fed with a ham hock he hitherto stood in the stable of allegory, on lines of force. Now he pulls up to pant his surprise opposed to Musikon's melodious voice.

But his anger is overwhelming. Before his breath can reach the rooftop, he bends back and lets go the seed of his manliness, which smells of jasmine and water roses.[46] The knees of the monster shake, rid of his force. It places its head on its paws, whining humbly. It breaks with its tail the wobbly vacation church of the people's trustees, who have reared it. And even this attack fails.

And while up on the airy mezzanine, amid Musikon's golden-flamed dances, umbala weia,[47] they bring out the last idol: Puppet Death—made out of stucco, fully stretched out in the car in order to be pulled up by strings. "Long live scandal!" shouts Pimperling as a salutation. "Poetic friend," so Toto, "a sickly desiccated corpse surrounds your head. Your eyes are colored cobalt blue, your forehead light ocher yellow. Give me the suitcase. Sela."[48] And Bridet: "Verily, silent master, you don't smell bad for your age. We're going to have one Hell of a good time. Let's each swing that dancing leg that he has torn from another.

45 The German *Hespar* presumably refers to *hesperidin,* a crystallizable substance found in the spongy skin of citrus fruit. *Aconite* is another term for the plant "wolf-bane" or "monk's hood," used to cure fevers or neuralgia.
46 The original reads *Wasserrosen* and what Ball clearly has in mind is an inversion of the term for rose water: namely, *Rosewasser.*
47 The chant *umba* constitutes a standard refrain in one of Richard Huelsenbeck's primitivist "negro poems."
48 The word *sela* means "crag" or "cliff" in Hebrew, though it is sometimes used in the Hebrew Bible as a place name, for instance, for Petra. A more likely interpretation is that Ball is thinking of *Shalom* (Hebrew) or *Salaam* (Arabic): a greeting and valediction.

Let's build a triumphal arch and wherever you place your foot may you be accompanied by blessings and praise."

Then Death nodded and took their experiences from them as one accepts a panegyric, and gave up his neck to the noose with which he was to be expedited into Hell. And they connected the pulley, turned the crank, and navigated him up. But the load was too heavy. Dangling and swaying, he reached three-fourths of the way into the upper sphere, vivified by the climb to the rooftop. Then the ropes tightened, sang, and whizzed. The wire crowed, and he crashed down from the dizzying heights and, with the impact of his full weight, hit the exceedingly honest Pimperling, who looked askance at such a jostling. Having been three times deceased and five times murdered, they carried him away from the road wrapped in a nose cloth and tried with great effort to push back into place the dislodged scaffolding of the back of his head. But nothing could be done. And even Death expired at Pimperling's death through death.

Then suddenly Mulche-Mulche uttered twelve resounding shouts, one after another. Her compass legs rose to the edge of the sky. And she gave birth. At first a little Jew,[49] who carried a tiny crown on his purple head and immediately climbed onto his umbilical cord and began to do acrobatics. And Musikon laughed, as if she were his cousin.

And forty days passed since Mulche stood chalky-faced at the guardrail of the mezzanine. Then she lifted the compass leg for a second time, high into the sky. And this time she gave birth to much swill, rubble, rubbish, ooze, and refuse. It rattled, clattered, and blustered over the guardrail and buried all the lusts and corpses of the plantigrades.[50] This pleased Jopp, and the Godhead lowered the butterfly net and looked surprised.

And another forty days passed during which Mulche stood thoughtfully with great gulping eyes. Then she lifted her leg for the third time and gave birth to Mr. Foetus, who is described on pagina 28 *Ars Magna*.[51] Confucius has praised him. A glittering edge runs across his back. His father is Plimplamplasko,[52] the high spirit, drunk with love beyond measure and addicted to miracles.

49 Several interpreters have suggested that a portrait of Tristan Tzara is intended here.
50 The term *plantigrades* describes beings, like humans, who walk fully upon the soles of their feet (*digitigrades* referring, on the contrary, to beings who walk upon their toes).
51 Though imprecise, the title *Ars Magna* may recall the work of the great Catalan logician and mystic Raimund Lull, on which hypothesis see Rechner-Zimmermann, *Die Flucht in die Sprache*, 163.
52 The name Plimplamplasko is borrowed from Maximilian Klinger's satirical novel *Plimplamplasko: Der hohe Geist* (Plimplamplasko: The High Spirit) (Basel: Thurneysen, 1780). Ball had wanted to publish a collection of his poems under this very title.

In the proportion as fear increases so too does laughter. The contradictions become glaring. Death assumes a magic appearance. Very consciously life, light, joy, are being defended. The higher powers personally step into the arena. God dances against Death.

One might have thought that Death himself had died, but far from it. No sooner had the great ghosts intoned their death lament on cement pipes, when lifted and put into motion by just such rhythms, than Death appeared sprightly again and began to dance on iron thighs. Clenching his fists inwardly, he beat the ground and stamped it with droning hooves.

53 The name Bulbo is based on the Latin word for "onion," an important detail inasmuch as Ball frequently imagined the personality as made up of layered onionlike skins, one grown over or under the next. In the course of the chapter, the Roast Poet's head is described as "a wonderful onion of spirituality."

And the great ghosts laughed and the casket lids of their cheekbones cracked. For the great dying was there again. Then Bulbo sank to his knees, threw his arms toward heaven, and cried:

"Deliver us, oh Lord, from enchantment. Pull, oh Lord, our festering mouths out from the garbage cans, gutters, and dumps where we lost ourselves. Have pity, oh Lord, on our presence in filth and latrines. Our ears are wrapped in iodine gauze, in our lung chambers graze crowds of wine beetles and the larvae of grubs. We have drifted into the realm of tapeworms and idols. The cry for dissolution prevails.

"With fiery sticks they beat our archangels. They lure your angels onto the earth and make them fat and useless. Where Hell borders paradise they roll their drunken kind into your promised land and the Wagnerian yodel resounds, wigalaweia, *in Germano panta rei*.[54]

"Your church has become a house of mockery and infamy. They call us blasphemers and toady Gnostics. Under the fullness of their flesh, however, appear their Apache and animal faces. How is one to love them? In the drawers the number of found foetuses increases and in the bed the lard head wallops.

"They no longer perceive the mummy in the hammock, the embalmed mess of limbs and the cholera bacilli in the seam of the bass violin. No longer the gruel that drips from the flue and the decaying mood of the father. They have already sold each other eternal life in the mother's belly.

"They traffic in wheat flour destined for your holy host and gargle their throats with a sour wine meant to represent your holy blood. You, however, forgive us our evils as we promise you to continue ours.

"I could of course dwell in some other time. But to what avail, oh Lord? Behold, I have consciously taken root among this people. As a hunger artist I nourish myself on asceticism. But the theory of relativity is not enough. Neither is the philosophy "as if." Our pamphlets no longer have any effect. The manifestations of the expanding marasmus multiply. Every one of the sixty million souls of my people ooze out from my pores. In front of you, oh Lord, it is rat sweat. But deliver us, help us, pneumatic father!"

Then there oozed out of Bulbo's mouth a black branch, Death. And they threw it into the midst of the ghosts. And Death exercised and danced up it.

Yet the Lord said: "*Mea res agitur* [This is my business]. He represents an aesthetic of sensuous associations that are connected with ideas. A moral

54 The Greek-Latin phrase is perhaps best rendered as "all things German" or "in Germany are all things."

13 **THE PINEAL EYE,** 1996, graphite and colored pencil on paper, 46 × 34 inches. Private collection, Berlin.

14 SATAN HOLDING HIS COCK, 1996, graphite and colored pencil and gouache on paper, 30 × 22 inches. Collection of the artist, courtesy of Matthew Marks Gallery, New York.

philosophy in grotesquerie. His doctorialness withers sweetly." And he too decided to dance, for he liked the prayer.

Then God danced with the righteous one against Death. Three archangels twist his hairdo into a towering toupee. And the Leviathan hung his back side over the sky wall and looked on. Above the Lord's hairdo, however, braided from the prayers of the Israelites, hovered the towering crown.

And a whirlwind arose and the devil crept into the secret quarters behind the dance floor and cried: "gray sun, gray stars, gray apple, gray moon." Then the sun, stars, apple, and moon fell to the dance floor. But the ghosts consumed them.

Then the Lord said "*Aulum Babaulum*, fire!"[55] and the sun, stars, apple and moon were flung from the intestines of the ghosts and took up their places again.

Then Death teased "*Ecce homo logicus* [Here is logical man]!" and flew to the upper step. And he opened up his great exhortation in order to prove his authority.

Then God hit him on the head with the Periodic Table[56] such that it shattered and continued to dance with manly flourishes and agile twists. The Periodic Table, nonetheless, was stamped out by Death before the ghosts consumed it.

Then Death made a rain of ashes from the black-sour of the shavings destined for coffins and clamored: "*Chaque confrère une blague, et la totalité des blagues: humanité*" [Every peer a joke, and the totality of jokes: humanity]. And with that he cracked the cover of his cheekbone coffins. But the shavings fell down all around and the ghosts consumed them.

Then God pointed the trumpet downward and called out: "*Satana, Satana, ribellione!*"[57] and there appeared the red man, his false majesty, who killed Death so that henceforth no man might recognize him. And the ghosts consumed him.

But behold, they became extremely powerful and shouted: "Let them hand us a roasted poet!"

"Cow, you are ours!" spoke the Devil.

"Liberty, fraternity, heaven, you are ours."

"Ourness and stinginess," spoke the Devil, "what does that mean?"

Then the Lord let them have the roasted poet. The ghosts, however, squatted down in a circle, degerminated him, peeled off his crust and light plumage, and consumed him. It was then discovered that his trouser buttons

---

55 *Aulum Babaulum* is a characteristically alliterative magical formula, like *abracadabra*.
56 The *Kategorientafel*, literally, the "table of categories."
57 The phrase derives from Giosuè Carducci's (1835–1907) famous *Inno a Satanà* (1865), a poem embraced by the champions of Italian national unification.

were consecrated wafers, that the Adam's apple was unfermented, the brain fragrant but built askew. And the youngest of the ghosts performed a eulogy:

"This was a psycho-fact," the speech began, "not a man. A hermaphrodite from head to toe. The spiritual shoulder stuck pointedly through the pads of his cutaway. His head a wonderful onion of spirituality. Blindly ruled by the urge to confess unhindered, his beginning, his end, and his origin were of such maidenly innocence, such uncompromising mental cleanliness, that we who follow in his wake have doubts regarding the revolutionary duty to morally uplifting motherhood, which cannot be reconciled with our still weakened striving toward a cosmos of flying will and surpassing of the earth—a necessary yet sweet problem within the tragedy.

"Glorious things lie buried alive here in a wild tangle of unsound and abstract rhetoric. Subjectivistic ecstatics were not always able to escape embracing a theatrical cause for its own sake. A stalwart fanatic and fakirlike salvation seeker, high priest and seer, source and impeller of dithyrambic drives, the only thing that impairs his fine example is that Max Reinhardt,[58] whose creative and rebellious direction fertilized the construction of singular visions, was able to bequeath his knowledge to the knowledgeable only after his death. *Requiescat in pace* [May he rest in peace]."

And they devoured him. And they devoured the speaker as well. And devoured the plates. And they devoured the forks. And the dance hall too. Oh, how good it was that the Lord had already left the scene. They would have also devoured him.

58 Ball's connections with Reinhardt (1873–1943), the great theater director, extended back to 1910, when Ball enrolled in his theater school, where he also briefly served as a part-time teacher. Ball subsequently parted ways with Reinhardt, so the reference here is sharply ironic. Not only was Reinhardt alive at the time the passage was written, but he was at the peak of his popularity.

There is nothing more to say. Perhaps more could be sung. "You magic quadrate now it's too late." So speaks one who knows the meaning of silence. "Ambrosian steer": which is understood as an Ambrosian song of praise. A leaning toward the Church is shown in vocabulary and vowels. The hymn begins with military reminiscences and ceases with an invocation to Solomon, that great magus who found comfort for himself by taking the Egyptian king's daughter to his heart. The Egyptian king's daughter is magic.

> You lord of birds, of dogs and cats, of ghosts and bodies, of specters and
>   grotesqueries,
> You above and below, on the right, on the left, ahead, about face and
>   halt,

The ghost is in you and you are in it. And you are in you and we are
    in we.

You are resurrected who was vanquished.

The unfettered one who rent his chains,

You are the almighty, the all-nightly, the resplendent, with a cauldron
    on your head.

In a welter of languages and toward the four winds, so is the thunder in
    your box burst asunder.

In reason and unreason, in the pale of death and the blush of rich life,
    are your towering nations.

In fire gullet and bullets' hail, in death sighs and endless curses,

In countless numbers of blasphemies, in clouds of printer's ink, host
    wafers and cakes.

So we saw you, so we held you, in a shower of faces carved from agate.

On fallen thrones on exploded cannons, on shredded newspapers, foreign
    exchange and records.

Colorfully dressed puppet, you hold the righteous sword above the
    tricksters.

You God of curses and of sewers, demon prince, God of the possessed.

You mannequin with violets, garters, perfumes and with the painted face
    of a whore.

Your seven youths pay off your truths, your great aunties are ruined,
    your cake is a red ball.

You prince of illness and medication, father of Bulbo and Tenderendas,

Of arsenic and salvarsans,[59] of revolvers, soaped rope and gas valves.

You loosener of all bonds, casuist of all quibbles.

You God of lamps and lanterns, you feed on light cones, triangles and
    stars.

You torture wheel, Russian swing of pain, homocentaurus, in flying
    pants through the sick ward you soar.

You wood, copper, bronze, tower, zinc and lead, an iron cock's vane
    whirring, you slide past.

You magic quadrate, now it is too late, you mystic quarter, Ambrosian
    steer,

59 As indicated by Green, salvarsan was an arsenic compound developed in 1910 by Paul
   Ehrlich for the treatment of syphilis, recurrent fever, and frambesia. It was sold under
   the trade label "606."

15 MACHETANZ, 1996, graphite and colored pencil on paper, 30 × 22 inches. Private collection, Zurich.

16 TWO CLOWNS AND A DONKEY, 1996, graphite and colored pencil on paper, 42 × 30 inches. Private collection, Mill Valley, Calif.

Lord who lays us bare, your five fingers are the fundament of our
salvation.

Lord of our hunt and kitchen Latin, lamentation drum of our existence,
eternalist, communist, Antichrist, oh! Most wise wisdom of
Salomo![60]

60 The reference is clearly to King Solomon, reputedly the wisest of men, yet Ball distorts
this into *Salomo* in the original typescript.

IX HYMN 2

It ought to be noticed how, in the second part of this hymn, a litany emerges out of buffoonery. The liturgical formulas dominate, to be sure. The voices and parties are still fighting, and consequently there is controversy concerning the thing from which one ought to be delivered.

> You who pushed aside our maids of honor,[61] our bouquets and perfumes,
>   our intoxicating drugs,
> With bombards, fifes and cymbals, with bright lights and verbiage we
>   salute you.
> You who threw our moon calves out into the street, our cookbooks and
>   astrologies,
> Who cried out with the voices of ten thousand changelings,

---

61 One of the typescripts for *Tenderenda* substitutes *Ehrenjungfrauen* (maids of honor) with *dargetonen Genitalien* (proper genital organs).

17 TOTO, WHO HAD HIS NAME AND NOTHING ELSE, 1997, graphite and colored pencil on paper, 27 × 20 inches. Collection of the artist, courtesy of Matthew Marks Gallery, New York.

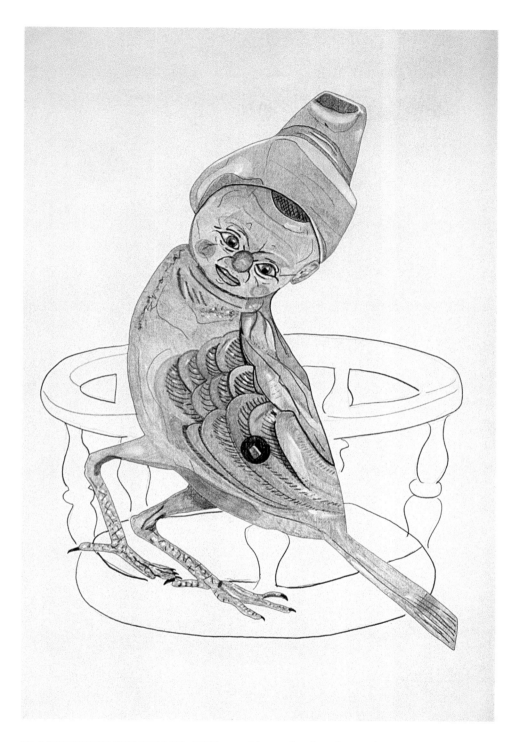

18 LILIENSTEIN IN THE DOCK, 1997, graphite and colored pencil on paper, 40 × 25 inches. Collection of the artist, courtesy of Matthew Marks Gallery, New York.

Who arrived and made his entrance, a laughing toy kite and triumphant
    one,
With coupons, tin, enamel, paper, and pin money we salute you.
You who in the cheek pockets of your horned head store scruffy children
    and zebras,
The dilly-dallying poet, the lukewarm proletariat, the newspaper man
    and the priest have given themselves for a single Mark.
Place the ring of your power through our noses and a fence around our
    jowls, tame our splendors.
We perform a great dance in clothes made from rags and paper, of
    windowpanes, tar paper shingles and cement.
We swing our all-German nobody walking sticks, painted with runes
    and swastikas.
Your realm lasts from the navel to the knees and the Lutheran codfish
    barks.
Deliver us, oh Lord, from the persecution of heretics and utopians, from
    adversaries and prophets.
Deliver us, oh Lord, from the pretensions of the theorycasters[62] and
    liturgists, from the united bell ringers.
Lead us away, oh Lord, from this land of duty bugs, of cold coffeecakes
    and places plastered with death certificates.
Stop beating with wood, copper, bronze, ivory, stone and other powerful
    drums.
Stop our dead from appearing and disturbing our warmth; for that, oh
    Lord, we implore you.
Cease placing ghosts on our table, in our coffee cups, and may no incubi
    rattle in the rafters of the staircase.

62 The original reads *Theoretikaster,* a neologism combining *Theoretiker,* or "theorist," with
    Aster, as in the flower, though there are other meanings implicit as well, such as "caste"
    (*Kaste*), "box," "barracks," or "cupboard" (*Kasten*).

X THE DIRECTOR OF DECAY

In this chapter it is assumed that a meat merchant will be the last one to be buried. However, it is later learned that a few others have survived the great death. The mourners are revenants and three-month-old corpses. The funeral turns out to be a ceremonial procession similar to the one that took place during the Eleusinian mysteries. To the right of the showplace, an oppressively felt darkness is being packed into boxes. To the left, the poets' club, which has likewise survived, is busily at work on registering the decay and appropriately minimizing the fantastic reality.

They were already in total agreement when the Director of Decay submitted his resignation. It was just the day on which the last burial had taken place. The deceased had assembled in full. They barely suppressed their stench, strapped tight their lower jaws, and passed perfume around. The horse cadaver that had to pull the hearse they wrapped in the vestments of the mass, so that his nakedness rich in worms would not show too obtrusively.

And the master of ceremonies, of the dark occurrences, raised his voice and read from the festival program:

"God, the almighty,
it has pleased him to call
unto him our ancestor, grandmother, mother and child.
Mr. Gottlieb Zwischenzahn
Of the firm Zwischenzahn, Kiefer & Co.,[63]
Sausage and Meat Wholesaler."

"He's gone here and there today," mumbled the choir.

"The departure of the deceased is exemplary. He was always a faithful servant to the Church. He is accompanied by expressions of dirty sympathy, the deeply felt expression of the pain of his relatives and friends who, rightfully recognizing the shifty situation, deserted him in time. And it should be added that the sausage factory, now inactive, was founded under the direction of the deceased."

Thereupon the funeral procession began to move, and the Director of Decay mounted the podium and conducted for the last time. And his famulus[64] made thunder on a baking pan. And as the smelly procession disappeared into the streets, one could hear the words of the corybants.[65]

"He who has landed at the dock late at night
Hardened and looking a fright,
With his beard, and his old man's
Leather wallet, always traveling—
Slaughterer of sheep and pig
Always doing mischief
Hinter and there he plies his own wares,
Expanding contracting,
His boorish soul he now fears
Are his dividends late?

63 The usual play with names is involved: *Gottlieb* (divine love); *Zwischenzahn* (tooth gap or between teeth); *Keifer* (jaw).
64 *Famulus* is a Latin term for "attendant" or "handmaid," usually in the service of a magician or scholar.
65 The corybants were priests of the goddess Cybele in ancient Phrygia; their rites were renowned for excessive revelry.

In his mind's eye does he blush?
He's gone to pot, he's gone to his fate."

And the priest stacked the remnants in the coffin together with a cross while the famulus was thundering and the Director of Decay was conducting.

"Carry him
flat on a hearse,
so that the corpse,
the busy one,
sucks nourishment and strengthens.
Place him on the skyfloor
Completely wrapped in percentages.
Button his vest less tightly,
He is climbing out of his trousers.
Delicately anoint his eyes
With all-German eagle's ink.
Above his tired head
Floats all that he profits."

Behold, one could see that the servants of the church of the lower heavens had gathered to the right. They wore cowls made of tolerant cashmere and tall caps of ashes and they were busy packing all available eclipses of the sun into wooden boxes. For the air was loaded down with them and causing headaches. Some of the very attendants of this black stratum had not covered their heads. Their tin eyes were crossed. Their tinder hair made of kindling wood rattled when caught by the wind as they were bending down.

To the left, however, the "Heavy Thigh" poets' club had posted its vibrators, powerful catapults that served to catch and to calculate the slightest oscillations in the life of the soul and its decay.

But they also had with them the washing machine of banalization, into which, from above, they stuffed reality in order to devaluate it with gear and churning stick. And since darkness was blinding everyone's eyes, some took the opportunity to indulge in wild erotic activities. They dragged up mud, mortar, and stones, and baked from them a gigantic vulva, the vagina of the goddess Ta-who-re.[66]

66 Ta-who-re plays on the name of the bloody battle that took place in Marne, France, in 1915.

19 ZIRRITIG-ZIRRIZITIG, 1996, graphite and colored pencil on paper, 25 × 39 inches. Private collection, Columbus, Ohio.

20 DENIZENS OF SATANOPOLIS CHASING THE JOURNALIST LILIENSTEIN, 1996, collage, graphite, gouache, colored pencil, and ink, 30 × 42 inches. Private collection, Oakland, Calif.

Then the Director of Decay lifted his arms three rungs higher, pointed toward the hot doings, and spoke: "Let the names and origins of these fellows be told."

And the famulus raised the baking pan like a black sun and said: "Be magnanimous, oh Lord, they are idealists. One can see it from their glowing life of the soul. They are born from twilight and have forgotten to die. Now they make poetry around the naked point."

And the Director of Decay again lifted his arms three rungs higher, blew his nose, spat to the right and left, and spoke: "Are there decadents among them? Transcendental decadents?"

"No," said the famulus, "there are boys of the night among them. They are climbing the monument to the father poet Gleim[67] and ruining the view."

And the Director of Decay took a closer look and said: "They seem to be involved in activities."

"Yes, Lord," said the famulus, "they are very much absorbed by their urges." He was alluding to the washing machine of banalization. At that moment one of the members of the large cohort left the magic circle, came closer, held out the sacrificial box and shouted: "Humanity in word and print! Priceless humanity!" And the others pushed closer, rang out the wet kerchiefs they had wound round their heads, and recited newly invented jokes and sayings.

The first: "Starry front of my suffering crown," and "Lamp king of Jerusalem." The other: "I have a point to make: soon, when you start your steep stair stepping . . . tread tripping . . . stair stairing." The third: "Tap, tap, my asthma, proceed, you carriage" and "behind our foreheads glow the great abscesses."

"You exaggerate, sir," replied the famulus. "Basically they are a harmless little folk. You must not honor them with your anger."

But when one in the back near the scaffolding began to smoke his pipe and read his essay "On the Beauty of Unlaid Eggs" out loud, the Director of Decay was overcome by impatience and shouted: "They are of course vulgar and provocative. They feel it beneath them to slave away. They want their place in the sun. Give them a penny for their collection, and a penny for the one who is blowing a song of lamentation on his windpipe. Serpents, scare them out of their holes. It pains me to see them sit thus."

67 Johann Wilhelm Ludwig Gleim (1719–1803) was known as Father Gleim owing to his generosity toward younger poets. He is principally remembered for his *Preussische Kreigeslieder von einem Grenadier* (Prussian War Poems by a Grenadier [1758]), which celebrate the campaigns of Frederick II.

Whereupon they protested. And discouraged, the famulus said: "They want to remain sitting here and consume their rind of greatbrain. Nothing more. Nor do they have their leggings any longer. They have sacrificed everything up to their shirts."

"Throw them the brown slacks of Abdul Hamid,"[68] said the master, resigned, "and let us continue. We cannot help them. Verily, the circumstance may arise, should tempers boil over, that they will come up with threats, place the sword against our stomach, because we made no attempt to buy up their experiences. By God, what an insolent species of man!"

68 Abdul Hamid II (1842-1918), the astute Turkish sultan who struggled to reform the Ottoman empire as it came under both increasing pressures from the West and regional revolts in Macedonia and Bulgaria. Abdul Hamid was always close to German interests and employed Germans for the reorganization of his army and finances.

Description of an elephant caravan from the world notorious cycle "gadji beri bimba." The author celebrated this cycle[70] **as a novelty for the first time in 1916 at the Cabaret Voltaire. At that time he wore a bishop's costume of glossy paper, with a towering blue-white shaman's hat, which to this day is being worshipped as a fetish by the mild inhabitants of Hawaii.**

> jolifanto bambla ô falli bambla
> grossiga m'pfa habla horem
> égiga goramen
> higo bloiko russula huju

69 First performed on June 23, 1916; this is the first of the two *Lautgedichte* (sound poems)
    anthologized in *Tenderenda.*
70 An earlier typescript read "this cycle of abstract sound strings" (*diesen Zyklus abstrakter
    Laureihen*).

82

hollaka hollala

anlogo bung

blago bung

blago bung

bosso fataka

ü üü ü

schampa wulla wussa ólobo

hej tatta gôrem

eschige zunbada

wulubu ssubudu ulu wasubada

tumba ba—umf

kusa gauma

ba—umf

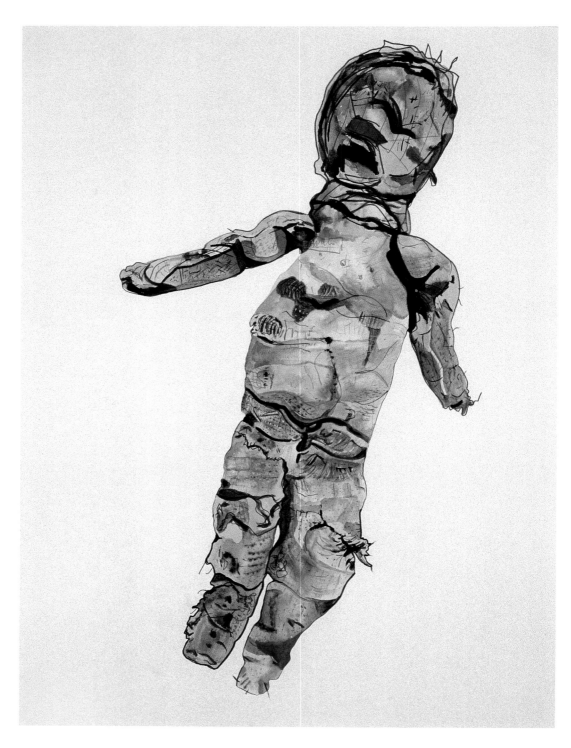

21 RAG DOLL, 1997, watercolor and graphite on paper, 30 × 22 inches. Private collection, Mill Valley, Calif.

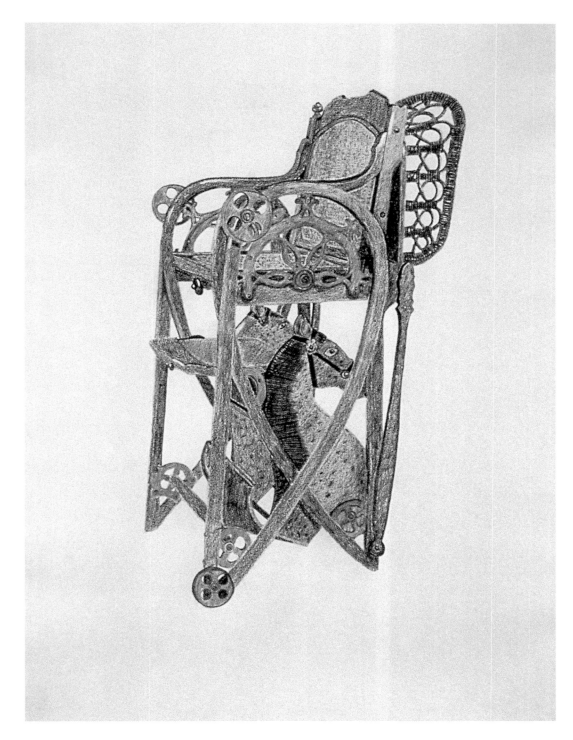

22 TRANSFORMING HOBBYHORSE I, 1995, graphite and colored pencil on paper, 19 × 27 inches. Collection of the artist, courtesy of Matthew Marks Gallery, New York.

Tenderenda, for his part, passes the homage on to his discreet consecration chieftain. The ancestor of hymnologists is in this hymn being called, among other things, "Chaldean archangel," "coral of the other world," and "master of fluidity." The fool's dance of this pamphlet is being offered up to him: "We distorter of faces, in firecoats, dancing around a water barrel." The last verses, in particular, reveal total devotion. Tenderenda is being seized by nostalgia for the hearth. During sad hours, he recites the verses for his own edification.

Chaldean archangel, aster king, purple
Man with hands meaning sleep
You make the animals appear in us
You attach us to the resounding order of magicians
You include us in the stars

Which cut us up and divide us.
Master of all saints, of all deceased
Glass of violas in which we have withered,
We die in width and breadth,
We contract the last cough,
We sink into eternal space, Laurentius—
Tears, shining and swarming.

You zone chief, black chief,
How addicted to falling seizures, to death throes we are!
The holy doctor Cosmas[71] cannot help us.
We die from you and toward you, we die completely.
In you are all things joined.
We bear the Big Dipper as a totem in our arms,
A sun of *terra sienna* upon our hearts.
Possessing by you possessed, we detach ourselves.

We tooth trumpet, fluttering in the crystal wind,
We tragic peacock, breaking on all steps,
We distorter of faces, in firecoats, dancing around a water barrel.
You belt of stars, you wall of orb, rolling darkness.
You oriental people, occidental people,
In a minor key mumbling war marches, foam around the Tower of
    Grace.

You *cymbalum mundi,*[72] coral of the other world, master of fluidity,
Out loud cry the scale of people and animals.
Out loud lament the people of the cities of fire and smoke.
Because your wonder-horns appeared, because you
looked at your earthen toys, because you inspected
your realm and us, the petty overseers of your assets.

71 Presumably an allusion to Cosmas of Alexandria, the sixth-century author of the
   Topographia Christiana, which argues for a vision of the earth as a flat rectangular plane,
   over which stretch the firmament and the heavens like vaulted ceilings.
72 The phrase *cymbalum mundi* means "world cymbal" and echoes the vision of the cosmos
   as a musical instrument maintained by various late antique esoteric and Neoplatonic
   sects. Indicative of Ball's wide-ranging reading habits, it more explicitly evokes the title of
   Bonaventure Des Périers's fierce attack upon Christianity in 1538, the *Cymbalum Mundi:
   Four Very Ancient Joyous and Facetious Dialogues.* The work was suppressed but
   reprinted in Paris later that same year.

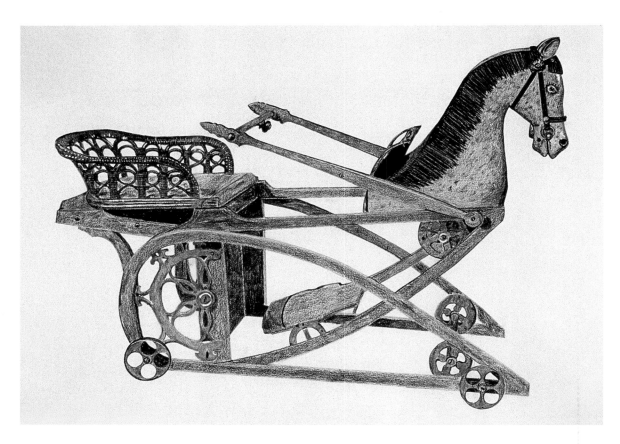

23 TRANSFORMING HOBBYHORSE II, 1995, graphite and colored pencil, 19 × 27 inches. Collection of the artist, courtesy of Matthew Marks Gallery, New York.

24 THE BIRTH OF MR. FETUS, KING OF THE JEWS, 1997, graphite and colored pencil on paper, 39 × 25 inches. Private collection, Mill Valley, Calif.

For the makeup cracked, the dice fell apart.
For nowhere was there such sin as here.

Your face pieced together by metaphors, Shrove-time poem puppet
Of our fears. You smell of white paper!
Page, ink, writing utensils and cigarettes,
We let everything lay. Meekly, we follow you.
From the numbers, which held us transfixed, our feet are loosened.
From the materials, which were burned into us, sweetness flows.
Rarities we exchange for cash, truth for vagaries.
One for two, and the night capital for Benares.

XIII LAURENTIUS TENDERENDA

Unabashed eruption or expectoration of the title hero. The author calls him a fantast and, in his eccentric manner, he calls himself "Church poet." He also describes himself as a "Knight of Glossy Paper," pointing to the Don Quixotish gear in which Tenderenda liked to move about during his lifetime. He admits to being tired of his mirth and implores the blessings of the heavens. Particular praise deserves the form of benediction, the cheerful tonal scale by which justice is done to Tenderenda's sky-dancing nature. Because he brings chimeras into the stable, he may be taken for an exorcist. The persecutions of the Devil, to which the benedictions point, are those *phantasmata* of which St. Ambrose has already complained, to be abjured, according to another saint, as a condition for entering into the order of monks. Otherwise Tenderenda's disposition is elegiac and shy of others. The wordplays, wonders, and adventures have softened him. He longs for peaceful quietude and the Latin absence.[73]

73 The German is a bit tortured here: "Er sehnt sich nach friedlicher Stille und nach lateinischer Abweseheit." Despite Ball's abiding love of and frequent recourse to ecclesiastical and liturgical Latin in *Tenderenda*, it underscores the work's larger call to go beyond (even Latin) words and recalls the "hunt and kitchen Latin, lamentation drum of our existence, eternalist, communist" alluded to in the concluding verse of Hymn I.

It began with a droning: Laurentius Tenderenda, the Church poet, a hallucination in three parts. Laurentius Tenderenda or the ranting interpreter of necessity. Laurentius Tenderenda, the quintessence of the astral cannonade. That was to be a prank delectable to eardrums. But it became a tragedy of sound human judgment and a farce for fashion daubers and word flagellators.

A producer of prayer books spoke the prologue, and the theater swayed with the whirling of the human crowd. The gables were secured with hat pins and from balconies hung the hungry tapeworms, elomen.[74] The dispositional body of Goliath was opened and ten stories fell out. The rattlesnakes were taken to the tower, and the buck's horn was blown for high tea.

Oh, this century of glowing light and barbed wire, primordial strength and abyss! What place do documents of torment hold here? Before a warrior people, before a gathered chorus of poetry editors? Laurentius Tenderenda or the missionary among the sweat foots and redskins of the Academy of Sports Training. A book of confessions and a coughing tower. I will offer up well-fed material. I am not inclined to bookish fights. If only there was not this constant death rattle of sulfur chloride. Not one step more, or it is my own death rattle.

Now they go to move their three-seater donkey, driving to a gallop. Garnets, lemon, and Venetian-blue smoke of their peaked hats. Now the hen broods at high mass, and they chase her with the alms bag. They cook their pocket watches in zinc salve and paint over Nostradamus with heliotrope.

For me it is veritable Satan's perfume. It also smells a little of pepper stew and pointed wire. In the second section the lamenters strap themselves again into stomach girdles of Koran passages. Art as buckle. Capuchin sermon in three installments. Or the encyclopedic prayer cylinder. Or the abysmal searching look into the infernal world of the mustached upheaval makers.

I would be a fine one, if I didn't catch on. A fine one I would be if I weren't willing to stalk the beast with bootjacks. The female ideal of the German people does not reside publicly in the house of lust. The cockatoo has fallen into poison. The blue rider is not a red cyclist. And I thought I had things bottled up.

They have put the squid on my bed. And given me their tooth roots to eat. Valerian has been my fare, and I have smoothed the church spire with sandpaper. And I know not whether I belong to those above or those below. For the unbelievable, the never-to-be-allowed, happens here.

74 As noted by Green and Meyer and Schütt, *elomen* is one of Ball's nonsense neologisms and occurs also in his noise poem *Wolken* (Clouds). The word appears Hebraic in inspiration, akin to names of God such as *Elohim.*

Without preamble: by nature I am a child of passion. My *mons puberis* knows to show itself with abandon. For forty days I find myself in soda. The long teeth of the godless grow in their jaws.

I could recite the psalms and make the sacred sign of the holy cross. Who would benefit therefrom? I could anoint my locks with sunflower oil and pluck at David's harp. *Cui bono* [To what end]? Portraying the bull-market men and master dyers of New Jerusalem: what use is that to me?

This is the eleventh and last of the parabases.[75] The Knight of Glossy Paper is weary of his joyfulness. The organ has coaxed his departure. The chimeras have been brought to their stalls and the Church father Origen[76] sunbathes his tonsure in the red sunset. Everlasting seeds, oh Lord, give us a good Cordial Médoc and silence for a moment the orchestra of triple-beaked water pipes.

Benedicat te Tenderendam, dominus, et custodiat te ab omnibus insidiis diaboli [May you bless Tenderenda, O Lord, and keep thee from all the trickery of the Devil].[77] *Oh Huelsenbeck, oh Huelsenbeck, quelle fleur tenez-vous dans le bec?* [What flower do you hold in your beak?].[78] The roots mate together in the sanctuary. Detectives are our cockades and we recite the "gadji beri bimba" as our nightly prayer.

Tenderenda the cross wielder shall come to be my name. It shall come to pass that on the *sedia gestatoria*[79] my bones shall be displayed. It shall come to pass that holy water shall be sprinkled over me. Full monk of preservation and filter cloth of uncleanliness shall come to be my name, ass king and schismatic. *In nomine patris et filii et spiritus sancti* [In the name of the Father, the Son, and the Holy Ghost].[80]

Luckily, my pentecostal humor has come through undisturbed by crass outsiders. Luckily, I am able to remain in good form. Had I a notebook handy or some other occasion offered itself, I would write down more of what comes to my mind. The whole time comes to my mind. It is a great downfall and falling down, this with fallen innocence allowed to be written down.

75 The parabasis was the principal choral part in ancient Greek tragedy.
76 Origen (185–254), considered the most distinguished early Christian theologian, was a Neoplatonist and ascetic (remembered for castrating himself in order to intensify his powers of contemplative concentration). His writings were among Ball's favorites in his late period.
77 A standard liturgical blessing personalized by Ball for purposes of blessing Laurentius.
78 The allusion is of course to Richard Huelsenbeck, author of *Memoirs of a Dada Drummer*, ed. Hans J. Kleinschmidt, trans. Joachim Neugroschel (Berkeley: University of California Press, 1991), and a close friend and collaborator of Ball.
79 A *sedia gestatoria* is a sedan chair, used for bearing important officials such as monarchs and popes.
80 Another standard formula derived from the Catholic mass.

25 THE ROASTED POET, 1997, linocut, 24 × 22 inches. Collection of the artist, courtesy of Matthew Marks Gallery, New York.

26 MULCHE-MULCHE IN LABOR, 1997, graphite and colored pencil on paper, 22 × 30 inches. Private collection, Miami Beach.

A magic incantation. It is intended for Tenderenda's two mystical beasts, the peacock and the cat. Two lofty bold and laconic beasts, the Jeremiah and wailing woman among the beasts. It is recommended that this passage be spoken lightly and not be dwelled upon for too long. It serves as a sort of clasp linking the last two texts.

baubo sbugi ninga gloffa
siwi faffa
sbugi faffa
ôlofa
fafâmo
faufo halja finj

sirgi ninga banja sbugi
halja hanja golja biddim

mâ mâ
piaûpa
mjâma

pâwapa
baungo
sbugi
ninga
gloffâlor

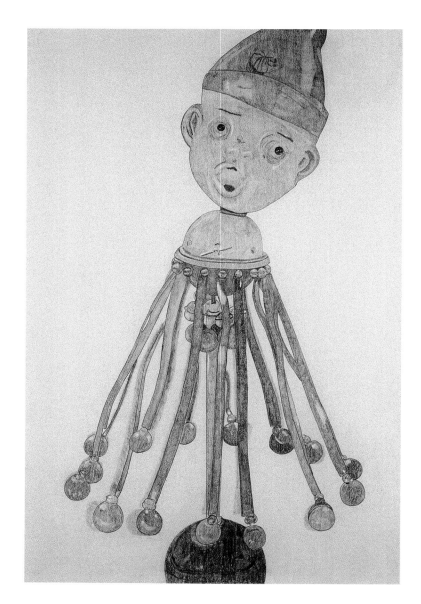

27 OVERWROUGHT WHIRLIGIG, 1996, graphite and colored pencil
on paper, 39 × 25 inches. Collection of the artist, courtesy of
Matthew Marks Gallery, New York.

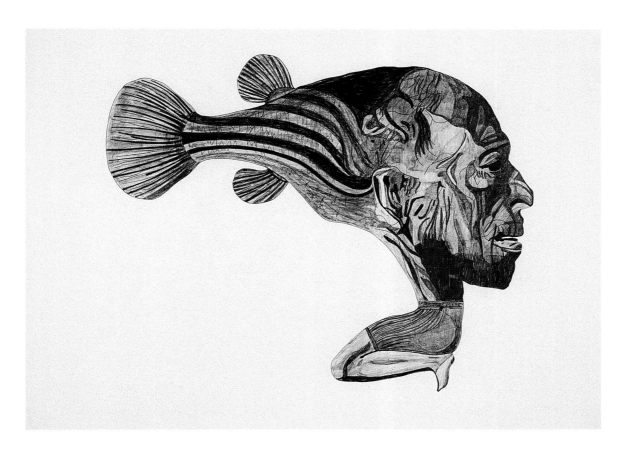

28 THE STUDY OF MAN #2, 1997, graphite and colored pencil on paper, 46 × 34 inches. Collection of the artist, courtesy of Matthew Marks Gallery, New York.

An astral fable. A kind of heavenly puppet play. Three segments allow themselves to be distinguished. The first: the Goldkopf couple witnesses a mystical occurrence. A white avalanche comes to call on them; toward them grows a heightened purity and brilliance. Their house sits above an abyss and upon the fabulous meadow where the alphabet tree ambles. This is that tree from which eat the poetic Adams and Eves. Delicate allegories assume bestial forms. Dream-like, the music-stands of laughter that Tenderenda dispersed during his lifetime. The second segment is the Ballad of Koko the Green God. The fantast's god. All blissful fortune derives from him so long as his wings flap in freedom. But, placed alone in captivity, he avenges himself by casting magic spells on those nearest him. The third segment is an epilogue for the Goldkopf couple. It shakes the dust of time from its feet and prophesies the end of the godless and the bewitched. The dance concludes, as is right and just, with a verse from Sir Poet Prince, Johann von Goethe.

81 Goldkopf means "gold head" in German.

Mr. and Mrs. Goldkopf light upon the blue wall. Mr. Goldkopf has a shooting star hanging from his nose. Mrs. Goldkopf has a green feather duster in her hat. Mr. Goldkopf bows low. Mrs. Goldkopf has a hand like a five-tined fork.

An avalanche comes up the stairs. Hard behind the night. A white avalanche up the teetering stairs. Mrs. Goldkopf curtseys. Mr. Goldkopf taps his brow. A white fountain springs from his head. In no other century had this been seen. Never in any century.

The fire-and-snow cocks fly up startled from the depths. The sore-throated cows wipe each other's noses. On the emerald meadow wanders the alphabet tree.

On the emerald meadow: soda-soap worm is bridled bucking. Its rider falls off and disperses the music stands of laughter. He mounts the morning and evening swing, rocks and swings and hops into the beyond.

Then come the flutebuck, the powderbuck, the tulipbuck, craning their necks. In the background stands a birdhouse. Inside sits a kaduda[82] cock and he is spuming stars.

Says Mr. Goldkopf in wonderment: "The tulip is a garden bloom, pretty, but without scent. On a hellish machine one cannot make coffee."

Says Mrs. Goldkopf: "*In gremio matris sedet sapientia patris* [The wisdom of the father lies in the bosom of the mother]. So it is with the tulip. Its bulb is planted in the earth. Accordingly, it's considered a bulbous root."

Says Mr. Goldkopf: "Epileptics fall from the trees all around. The blue pipe of the mighty siphon lures. The image of the sacrosanct Trinity glows above the alphabet tree. Are you not astonished, Mrs. Goldkopf, by the height of childishness reached by all the goings-on?"

Says Mrs. Goldkopf: "Oh, you with your fanatic all-impetuous ideas! We are dancing beasts in towering headgear. We grapple with sobriety. Fruitlessly so. Who knows anything about anyone?"

And Mr. Goldkopf: "Yet do you recall Sambuco?[83] Five houses on a green wall. The ground on which you stand: triangular glass shards in outer space. Koko the Green God has bewitched us."

And Mrs. Goldkopf: "Koko, that is, our son? Why do you want to play *Weltschmerz* [world weariness]? Your distance and melancholy, your precocity

82 The German original reads *Kaduderhahn*, the adjective *kaduder* being a neologism probably based upon the Latin *caudatus* (with a tail), though a reference to *caudeus*, or "wooden," may also be intended.

83 *Sambuco* is so described in *Flight Out of Time* (178): "I was in the Ticino (Melide) for some time and would very much like to live in this heavenly countryside forever. You go over the Naret Pass down to the Maggia Valley. Sambuco: an emerald dream; in the evening among deserted huts a fisherman stood with his long rod. The mountain lake near the crystalline peaks: transparent in its icy depths."

and experience; only to think of it! Mouth, brow, and eye sockets buried in saffron. What are your complaints?"

STROPHE

Koko the Green God once flew freely
above the marketplace in the kingdom of Sambuco.
But then he was caught and put behind a rough wire fence
and fed with pomade and with the undergarments of old women.
He gave no answer to the insulting query as to his condition.
He no longer predicted the fate of what comes next and beyond the next
    world.
Grieved and lonely he sat on his dowel.
The blessings of his presence flourish no more.
No more does the violet clapping of his wings radiate through the world.
His shrunken face became that of an old lady owl.
And he led an absolutely logical existence replete with paralysis.
Shaken at night by the impregnating insanity of the stars,
He avenged himself by bewitching those nearest to him.

ANTISTROPHE

Light him revolting light!
Sun of death, inflate the gables of the filthy Bumbu who took him
    captive.
Let his ballad be played in all the mouth organs of modern times.
Let the streets be well upholstered for his return.
May the twelve zodiacal signs live by his glory.
The chief bigwig is allowed to spend the night with his sister-in-law as a
    reward,
Humans and beasts shed their clothing of body and woes,
When he returns from the clutches of the bandy-legged robbers.
For him his mother has set out with bared talons here and beyond
For him his father cradles the spirits of evil in his hand.
He has abandoned us and built living images of our torments.
He has come to break the spell that besets us.

MRS. GOLDKOPF: "May it come to pass."
MR. GOLDKOPF: "When Metatron[84] stomps through the firmament."

84 *Metatron* figures among the titles assigned to the supreme order of angels in Jewish gnosti-
    cism.

MRS. GOLDKOPF: "It shall come to pass that he will seize the four ends of the earth and shake out the godless."

MR. GOLDKOPF: "Calm yourself, Madam, if you please. Let us mount the colorful ass and ride across the precipice in leisurely fashion."

MRS. GOLDKOPF: "One moment, if you please, so that I can seize the sun, this abscess, with fire tongs and assign him to the higher path."

CHORUS SERAPHICUS

The whole and total shall now come to pass.
Through the death dance it strives for allegory.
The unheard-of at this time steps in.
In glaring light: the depraved.[85]

85 The passage plays off of the "Chorus Mysticus" from Goethe's *Faust:* "Alles Vergängliche / Is nur ein Gleichnis; / Das Unzulängliche / Hier wird's Ereignis; / Das Unbeschreibliche, / Hier ist's getan; / Das Ewigwibliche / Zieht uns hinan." Cited from Wenzel-White, *The Magic Bishop,* 152.

29 BOUND AT GOLGOTHA, 1998, watercolor, gouache, and graphite on paper, 85 × 30 inches. Collection of the artist, courtesy of Matthew Marks Gallery, New York.

30 THE VIOLET-FACED SEER IN THE WHIRLPOOL OF BIRTH AND DEATH, 1998, colored pencil on paper,
60 × 36 inches. Collection of the artist, courtesy of Matthew Marks Gallery, New York.

F<small>ORM</small>A<small>T</small>I<small>VE</small> ESOTERICISM

<small>IN</small> <small>ZU</small>RICH DADA

A Revisionist Reading of *Tenderenda the Fantast*

JONATHAN HAMMER

As *Obadiah's* was a mix'd case, —mark, Sirs, —I say, a mix'd case; for it was
obstetrical, —*scrip*-tical, squirtical, papistical, —and as far as the coach-horse was
concerned in it, —caball-istical—and only partly musical; . . . .

—But here, you must distinguish—the thought floated only in Dr. *Slop's* mind,
without sail or ballast to it, as a simple proposition; millions of which, as your
worship knows, are every day swimming quietly in the middle of the thin juice of
a man's understanding, without being carried backwards or forwards, till some
little gusts of passion or interest drive them to one side.

—Laurence Sterne, *Tristram Shandy*

A fixation with dark filth and luminous purity structures the art and life of Hugo Ball. Ball sought both to cleanse the world of the historical burdens of his time and to absolve his own homosexual guilt through fervor. His quirky obsessions bespeak a gnostic universe of good and evil, a universe in which he vied for peace by interchangeably embracing anarchism's hyperindividualism and promises of mutual succor, on the one hand, and by abandoning himself to mysticism, on the other. Ball's itinerary was polar. But apostasy to mysticism became his final calling. When the sodality of DADA, with its promises of a definitive dismantling of artistic rear-gardism, failed to provide him with the societal and sexual healing he craved, he discarded it for an antipodal asceticism.

Ball was already leaning heavily in this direction, as is evident throughout his short-lived DADA adventure. His sound poetry and his fantastic novel *Tenderenda* abound with expressions of Kabalistic, Rosicrucian, and Manichean thought. Careful study reveals how prevalent these trends were from Zurich DADA's inception.

Can DADA, with its lawlessness and reliance upon naive systematics, adopt a Kabalistic vocabulary and attain the "cleaving of thought," a pious ascent to a "union of the soul" with the ineffable, that results through recitation and invocation into things blessed and augmented? A revisionist reading suggests that it can. Thus, the famous photo of Ball in costume at the Cabaret Voltaire provides more than a portrait of the artist as Grand Master of Ceremonies; it shows Ball in costume as Sanctified Seer.

On that occasion, Ball recited what he referred to as a magic "incantation" from the "gadji beri bimba" cycle. He proffered sound poetry from a Kabalistic standpoint.

For Ball, the poem-incantation not only gives voice to a purer, more "honest" form of expression but above all taps into a metalinguistic form of expression, or "cleaving." In the language of Kabala, thought returning to its source becomes identical with it. Just as water returns to water, so utterance returns to itself in Ball's sound poems. Union with the ineffable is achieved by the psycholinguistic superiority and purity of sound poetry. Although the intellect remains tied to physical matter, it delves to a deeper substratum wherein it can articulate a greater and more exact expression.

In the opening chapter of *Tenderenda*, "The Rise of the Seer," the artist-seer strives for divine spirit in order to attain prophetic power and to unfold the events of the future (which the artist-Ball achieves using the device of a prefatory paragraph). He is able to overcome and thwart the intentions of the populace of the imaginary city inasmuch as, in Kabala, the closer one comes to achieving union, the less one is affected by the thoughts of others, whether honorable or contemptuous. His desire is fulfilled: in fact, the Seer does literally rise. He preaches to and extols a citizenry made up equally of the cognoscenti and the vulgar. He attempts to provide guidance toward a higher union by setting before them the letters of the divine name: DADA. By meditating upon this equivalent of the tetragrammaton, he insists, the soul achieves enlightenment. Ball's chanting and rejoicing in the divine name at the Cabaret Voltaire is therefore cast in the mold of the Seer in *Tenderenda;* they are interchangeably transmogrified. As with the rise of the Seer, the event at the Cabaret is meant to precipitate cleaving to DADA.

The state of meditation upon the tetragrammaton referred to in Kabala as *devekut* is a premystical union wherein exceptional contact with higher entities is available and prophecy possible.[1] First the spirit mounts, then it returns to its source, and then it mounts even higher. There are many such ascensional moments in *Tenderenda.* Characters lift off, overleap landscapes, and metamorphose into birds, all in direct relation to acts of prophecy.

Devekut allows Ball to create a multifaceted literary alter ego. As he lives his DADA adventure, he simultaneously writes *Tenderenda* in an oracular vein, unfolding events both as literature and prophecy. His style is one of truncation and encryption. Ball the mystic meditator finds the highest forms of expression in silence and hope, his consciousness infused with a sense of the power of the word and by his own verbal impotence. The sound poems are therefore invocations of a lost place between language and thought. For in Kabala, the "true" spoken word serves to interpret between the speaker's heart and that of the listener.

Ball unfolds his prophetic narrative as foreordained autobiography. In the Romantic tradition of the *Erziehungsroman* (a genre that charts the protagonist's gradual enlightenment), Ball, with the sweeping gestures of a Dante and the intimacy of a Novalis, prefigures for the reader a future world of doom. Is it not poignant, after all, that the Zurich Dadaists were hardly more than children whose learning adventure was characterized not by educated innocence but by the crushing realization and horror of war?

Ball is prescient regarding the imminent destruction of European culture, because he believes European culture has already been destroyed. His lens on the present is the lens of the past. Hence his likening of the Prague of Rudolf II to the great wave of spiritualism that gave birth to modernism and his conviction that the Elector Frederick's attempt to preserve the glory of the Renaissance presaged DADA's salvific crusade. Against this historical backdrop Ball casts himself in a retrospective role. For him this past is a time of "the cult of genius, the cult of the unique and of the creative, the Shakespeare mania," and the present is but a reprise.[2] His DADA landsmen are the latter-day counterparts of the followers of Christian Rosencreutz, destined to be driven underground in the face of a new Thirty Years' War and to incumbent annihilation. Conceived within the fold of a language of war and failure, DADA was fated to die even as it was born. Of this Ball was certain. For he envisioned his autobiography as rooted in history and written backward, from death to birth.

Ball views creation and individuation as a circular process. This circularity is a defining attribute of esotericism. It is a pastoral tenet of thought that folds back upon itself, decoding and encoding so as to render the system an initiatory conundrum. Ergo, nothing can come to be without foreknowledge of its own existence. We are born fully formed by experiences within, which are then meted out, in a finite series, the last of which coincides with death and the depletion of all we know. Hence, Ball's distinctive sense of prophetic vision. A seer is inhabited by memories of a future foreseen. He bears witness to eternity exposed to the caprice of many possibilities, oppressed by endless combinations. Past and future run parallel courses. One extends from birth to death and uses intellect as the means to gather knowledge. The other extends from death to birth and conveys already-developed intrinsic instinct. This is a specifically human capability, the result of our bifurcated brain lobe. One lobe allows for empirical cognition; the other perpetuates instinctual processes.

At the Cabaret Voltaire, Ball stages this division in the guise of the signifier *Aleph.* He figures as the tarot magus: the left arm (that of alchemy) possesses the baton with which to enact magic, ascending in cosmic query; the right arm roots earthbound. In Ball's conception of DADA, creation consists in the coupling of these arms, lobes, timelines (death to birth, birth to death).

Randomness, innocence, and the debris generated by human existence inform each life. Does the artist forge a style in linear fashion, one piece built on the existence of the piece before it? Or is the first piece a cryptic seed from which all subsequent work develops, affording a more palatable and reductive reading of the original? From one perspective, we see a sustained shaping, a maturation process; from another, a complex and complete entity that, though continuously exploded and explicated, always remains one. The esoteric crystallization of the fusion of multiplicity and singularity is the "body of work" that for Ball necessarily assumes the form of autobiographical narrative.

Such a reading raises ontological questions regarding the nature of the art object. In so doing it sets out to provide more than an a priori argument regarding the unfolding of events. It puts forward an a priori *puzzle,* in which the contemplation of overlaps opens new vistas. Ball's preoccupation with a return to the *primary source* is not reducible to questions of historiography. Far from "scientific," his views deliberately assume the form of a prophetic riddle based upon misunderstandings and misinterpretations. They do so in the name of a new truth consistent with other formative epochal trends in thought. Modernism, as Ball experienced it, was born of a syncretism between divergent paradigms in thinking and convergent past- and future-oriented impulses. So, with ease and glee, Ball recognizes precedents for his own avant-gardism in previous eras such as Hellenism and the Renaissance.

Let us return to the photograph of Ball in costume at the Cabaret Voltaire. This frequently reproduced and familiar image captures a seminal moment in the history of modernism: seminal not least because of the degree to which it contributes to our own experiential self-framing. In his strange attire he brings to the forefront the role of the surrogate, the simulacrum, the self-portrait. He instantiates the vision of, and preoccupation with, oneself as body and symbol, as a being of mutualities both flesh and blood and allegorical. At once dour and mirthful, Ball's self-mockery provides a first layer of critique: that of irony. His ritual is no less camp than those staged by Crowley and Mathers. His hand is transformed, a tool with which to enact his "natural" magic. His dunce's cap becomes a philosopher's stone to mitigate the cosmic yearning of his pineal eye. His cape and vestments are the sacrificial garb worn by the priest at the moment of consecration. Paralyzed, he is frozen rigid in a moment of religious meditation, a convocation of his roles as performer, initiate, and visionary.

Devekut is not only a state out of which prophecy is born but is also closely connected with notions of ritual sacrifice understood in psychological terms. As Ball blesses, so he self-sacrifices. Recurrent in *Tenderenda* are many such examples of immolation and destruction through prophetic pronouncement. Since Ball conceived DADA as a sodality of healing in a Rosicrucian sense, his devekut meditations are more than personal experiences. They are public actions, gestures addressed to the community.

Like their Rosicrucian counterparts, DADA manifestos and manifestations sought provocation and publicity. In the Rosicrucian manifesto *The Discovery of the Fraternity of the Most Noble Order of the Rosy Cross,* the birth of a healing brotherhood skilled in Kabala is so described: "After this manner began the Fraternity of the Rose Cross; first by four persons only, and by them was made a magical language and writing, with a large dictionary which we yet daily use to God's praise and glory, and do find great wisdom therein."[3] Later comes a description of the primary mission of this brotherhood: "Their agreement was this: First, that none of them should profess any other thing than to cure the sick and that *gratis*."[4] In weighing the impact of these utterances upon Ball, we should recall how deeply steeped he was in the legends and history of the Palatine (his birthplace) and in the role of his father, known for his storehouse of fairy stories based upon historical incident. There is also the matter of Freemasonry, the practical branch of Rosicrucianism. Ball writes in his diary that German classical literature embraces Masonic notions in an attempt to create a secret society able to combat obscurantist nationalism and to foster intellectual and moral forces congenial to the emancipation of humanity. DADA and Freemasonry were associated through Von Laban on the Monte Verità. Finally, in *Tenderenda* the name of Solomon is invoked as the "father" of Freemasonry associated with the apocryphal birth of architecture and the building of the first temple.

The above-cited passage from the Rosicrucian manifesto is also pertinent to the debate over the origin of the word DADA. This issue has been argued with vehemence and ambiguity over the past half century. In my view, the word was indeed coined by Hugo Ball. In the July 28, 1915, entry to his diary, Ball refers to the chapter in *Tenderenda* entitled "Johann the Carousel Horse." Can there be any doubt that the rocking horse—or rather, the surrogate carousel horse—that surfaces here as a mascot for the "Blue Tulip" group of visionary poets (not unlike the blue rose of Romanticism depicted in the great educational novel *Heinrick von Ofterdingen*) provides an uncanny personification of the idea of DADA? The publication of this chapter of *Tenderenda* predates the opening of the Cabaret Voltaire by half a year and places Ball firmly at the inception of Zurich DADA's remotest precursor. (Furthermore, at the time there was a popular hair tonic on the market in Zurich bearing the brand-name DADA. The same company also manufactured lily-milk soap, which corresponds with Ball's alter ego character in *Tenderenda* : the Journalist Lilienstein. In Ball's "First DADA Manifesto," he writes: "DADA is the world's best lily-milk soap. . . . DADA Mr. Anastasius Lilienstein.")

The much documented dictionary story concerning the actual discovery of the word DADA is directly related to the above-quoted Rosicrucian manifesto. Huelsenbeck writes: "Hugo Ball sat in an armchair holding a German-French dictionary on his knees. . . . I was standing behind Ball looking into the dictionary. Ball's finger pointed to the first letter of each word descending the page. Suddenly I cried halt. I was struck by a word I had never heard before, the word

DADA."[5] Ball alludes to the episode in his first manifesto. "DADA," he confirms, "comes from the dictionary."[6]

I believe that Ball equated the word DADA with the tetragrammaton, the letters D A D A corresponding to the Hebrew letters *yod, hey, vov,* and *hey* that comprise the holy name *Yahweh.* Ball conceived of DADA as a password, as a way to attain access to the ineffable through meditation, as a Kabalistic method (uninformed by actual Kabalistic doctrine) to further his vigorous work of prophecy, self-sacrifice, and cultural healing.

I view Ball's life up until his apostasy as a threefold path of gnostic Manichaeism, Rosicrucianism, and DADAism. Manichaeism frames its omniscient images of world creation and development within a stark duality of light and dark, much like that embraced by Ball in *Tenderenda,* whose brooding and powerful imagery is laced with gnostic anguish. Ball is explicit on this point, as when he likens the DADA group to a gnostic sect, writing: "There is a gnostic sect whose initiates were so stunned by the image of the *childhood* of Jesus that they lay down in a cradle and let themselves be suckled by women and swaddled. The Dadaists are similar babes-in-arms of a new age."[7] An induced regression to childishness is a key motif in DADA, linked in Ball's case to his theories concerning sound poetry. Childhood is an age where precognitive thought and linguistic development merge into a lucid and unencumbered expression—in this case sound poetry, which inhabits the realm of play. It is here that egocentric thought is fully enacted. For Ball, this reveling in artificial innocence is a mystic act of atonement. In "Johann the Carousel Horse" he describes the guileless wanderers traversing a landscape of signs and omens toward an empty horizon. They are innocents, child romantics, and untainted naïfs.

If, as Ball writes, DADAism is like a gnostic sect, one need look no further than *Tenderenda* for a text pregnant with some of the most common themes of Mandaean poetry. In each of its prose chapters, for example, the novel evokes characters clearly "alien" or "other." The outsiders—recognized as such by those around them—combine the dual traits of superiority and suffering that recur in all of Ball's alter egos: the Seer, Machetanz, the journalist Lilienstein, Bulbo, and the like. The "other" is a bearer of the world of light and, according to gnostic doctrine, is at once all-knowing and persecuted. (This literary tradition exposes one of the first of many sources for Ball's complex beliefs regarding the "modern artist" and his or her societal role as both villain and child.)

The gnostic theme of one "beyond" or "without" this world is ubiquitous in *Tenderenda.* In the first chapter, we are already transported to an imaginary city with imaginary inhabitants. This tendency in Ball's work to favor landscapes outside the real world strips the latter of its potential for achieving wholeness, and subsequently peace. Instead the unreal world looms as a forbidding devil-place, such as in the chapter "Satanopolis," a city driven by compulsions and neurotic tendencies.

Multiple worlds denote a pluralism, with life a battered vessel that must forever travel the cosmos without deviation. It is a gnostic universe; each world is equally demonic and each world is equally collective. So, when Ball's characters travel from one world to another, they are wanderers seeking escape through a maze of systems ruled by darkness, where the life of the other has been condemned to feel pain without redemption. This is the world in which Ball finds himself. His pathology manifests itself through his characters in two ways: they are all ultimately the same, and they are all autobiographical. His real-life example thus sets the stage for prophecy. The close coupling between the real and the suprareal provokes frequent time manipulation.

The novel's context is both ancient and futuristic, creating a feeling of queasy instability, a sense of exile and alienation. Characters assume spatial as well as narrative proportions. The Devil becomes his own city. The Seer's flight produces geographic dislocation. The monster is as great in size as "The Grand Hotel Metaphysics." But even in the midst of this chaos, Ball upholds tenets of Manichaeism, wearing a gentle mantle in the face of evil. He endeavors to act with a "force of light" that can redeem the human soul from the "force of darkness."

In "Satanopolis" the journalist Lilienstein dwells in the moon house. Gnosticism interprets a dwelling as the surrounding upon which life depends. A given dwelling may be abandoned, but only for another. For without one, a person's sense of nakedness would be overwhelming. Accordingly, an inn or hostel is a place wherein "aliens" dwell communally, forming a transient world in which the inhabitants are viewed not as guests but, instead, as permanent habitués. The inn metaphor in gnostic language also summons up the specter of the body, itself envisaged as the soul's hotel. Aliens such as Musikon and Toto ("who had his name and nothing else") inhabit "The Grand Hotel Metaphysics" along with Mulche-Mulche, whose body-hotel gives birth to DADA, the crowned Jew, or the name of the ineffable.

Gnostic images of dispersal and splintering also abound. Breaking and explication—in life, in autobiography, in characterization—describe a common habit of Ball's thought. His quest for a place of purity and state of peace untainted by neurotic guilt, manifest in sound poetry and resulting in Kabalistic union, figures as a pursuit of light. But in *Tenderenda* darkness returns, ever incursive. Characters splinter and fracture; descriptions of decimations and cuttings parallel DADA's own rituals, espoused in poetic methods and collage techniques. When things fragment, they become multiple worlds of darkness to which the artist is banished. Salvation hinges upon piecing back together that which has been scattered. It is attained through the act of ascetic conversion effected by purging oneself of evil and embracing spiritual and physical cleanliness. As such, Ball's thought and actions from the DADA period until his death were never at odds with the long tradition of hermetic Catholicism extending from Plotinus to Porphyry to Augustine to Ball. Porphyry writes: "Endeavor to ascend into thyself, gathering in from the body all thy members which have been dispersed and scattered into multiplicity from that unity which once abounded in the greatness of its power. Bring together and unify the inborn ideas and try to articulate those that are confused and to draw into light those that are obscured."[8] Think of Ball in costume at the Cabaret Voltaire, gathering together through sound poetry his psychological world "scattered into multiplicity."

Here we have a sharpened contrast between levity and gravity, light and dark. Devices for raising the soul and spirit into the light such as Ball's sound poetry and his contemplation of the word DADA as tetragrammaton are pitted against the oppressive vocabulary of falling and capture that recurs in varied guises throughout *Tenderenda*. Each time a character in the novel begins a successful ascent, he is made to fall and is subsequently captured—both common gnostic themes. The last line of the chapter "Laurentius Tenderenda" reads: "It is a great downfall and falling down, this with fallen innocence allowed to be written down." Life is cast down from the freedom of light into an alien world of dissimilitude. The body becomes a cage. Reduced to bones, Laurentius Tenderenda will be enshrined and displayed on the papal litter, the *sedia gestatoria*. Machetanz's sentence is to eat his own self-ground flesh. Here again Ball's language is reminiscent of that found in a gnostic text: "They have let me alone in this world of evil ones. . . . He is overcome with the fear and desolation of loneliness. . . . The evil ones conspire against me. . . . Day in day out I seek to escape them."[9] Lamentation is frequent in Ball's writings, as is groping for that which lies just beyond reach. Characters are infected with the poison of darkness: in Machetanz's case, reduced with a numbness and unconsciousness that renders him ignorant and breeds a despair so great that it precipitates his untimely demise. Such gnostic fantasies as being devoured by demons occur again and again in Ball's DADA writing. His intoxication both in the cabaret and in *Tenderenda* betokens the ignorance of the world, with its endless noise, a drunkenness induced by an always claustrophobic pandemonium. Although *Tenderenda* is short, Ball conjures up space with remarkable density thanks to stylistic dislocations and tortuous language of gnostic inspiration. Nowhere is this done to greater effect than in his portrayal of the reception that awaits his "alien" men in the "world down there," whether within the novel, as with the journalist Lilienstein, Bulbo, and the rest, or in his own life, as recounted in the diary. Other aliens exalt and welcome the arriving alien as one of their own. They understand his alien ways and his alien speech. But the cosmic "world up there" is shocked and surprised, for there forces do not comprehend the phenomenon in their midst. Finally, there are the contemptuous inhabitants who vilify the alien. To quote the Mandaean text that almost exactly parallels the plight of the journalist Lilienstein: "What has the stranger done in the house, that he could found himself a party therein? We will kill the stranger. . . . We will confound his party, so that he may have no share in the world. The whole house shall be ours alone."[10] A similar raid is launched by the populace to oust the strange inhabitants of the Grand Hotel Metaphysics. This conflictual nature is one aspect of Ball's model of the relationship between the artist-alien and the world and its inhabitants. The gnostic notion of successive incarnations of opposites that complement one another, assuming the form of legendary characters such as Gilgamesh and Enkidu, lay the foundation for Ball's personality disorder. His complex consists of a dual incarnation within a single soul. Ball's quest as a Manichean initiate is to parry darkness (the shadow of good every time good is done) with gentleness. To practice gentleness in the face of evil is a key gnostic task, for love is understood as the redeemer of the human soul. So why did Ball tire so quickly of his DADA adventure? Perhaps he saw the balance tipping toward violence, away from love. Perhaps he was unable to reconcile DADA with his particular vision of healing based on the understanding of the alien-artist as prophet-seer attaining contemplative union with the ineffable light.

This quest for the grail that contains light and warmth is familiar in early modernism, formulated in the common language of fin-de-siècle spiritualism, a language that begets syncretic misunderstanding and deliberate distortions. Whether borrowing terms from theosophy, anthroposophy, Freemasonry, psychoanalysis, Rosicrucianism, or alchemy, both modernist writing and the visual arts regularly use the image of the pineal eye, which functions not only on a cosmic level but also on the level of sexual exploration of the body and orgiastic yearnings. The pineal gland (or third eye) is depicted as the organ by means of which humans can connect directly with the cosmos. In a previous evolutionary stage, humankind was possessed of an organ visible at the top of the head, which although altered in appearance over the course of eons, is still detectable in our own epoch. The pineal gland, our fontanel or soft spot, now exists in an exposed form only in our embryonic stage, after which it is covered by the brain. It is the organ that allows for the perception of temperature, the nuances of warmth and cold. As both metaphor and physical reality, toward warmth we are drawn, just as from cold we recoil. Figuratively speaking, our temperature sense is the mechanism of human inquiry. It provides the means by which the soul goes forth to meet the world of light, the sun. In alchemy this sense is symbolically materialized into the pseudo object of the philosopher's stone, a conduit between humankind and the cosmos. Through such a mediation, the plantigrades of our world can recapture the link with our future evolutionary selves described by Plato (in terms that Ball echoes in *Tenderenda* as past-future landscapes), as past descendants of the Atlantean era.

Third-eye imagery is pervasive in the history of art. Traditional Indian art contains a mythological incarnation of Shiva as a *linga*, or the phallic symbol of god. An *ekamukha* type of linga is a "one face," the head of Shiva with a third eye on top of the phallus—the third eye here related to omniscience. In Coptic religion, scripture in the form of a large codex was carried in processions on top of the priest's head. The scripture itself became the philosopher's stone, as language, housed in a book for initiates, in turn houses and channels the human impulse to query and learn. Then, of course, there is the third eye of Freemasonry atop the pyramid on the dollar bill.

Ball's venture into sound poetry must also be viewed as the probing of a type of scripture made up of magical incantations hurled at a mesmerized public. It provided him with an oracular model of prophecy to which access is gained through deep contemplation. It also serves as the preacher-seer's arm of power and control. Just as Ulysses is condemned to Hell in Dante's *Inferno* for his powers of persuasion—Ulysses leads his men on a fruitless voyage of adventure, essentially betraying the true homeland—so Ball the magician at the Cabaret Voltaire aims to captivate by wielding language. In his diary, Ball confirms his understanding of the word as *logos* (truth and power). He was aware that glamour and grammar share a common etymological root, aware that to cast glamour over a crowd is to cast a spell. He thought written language a *grimoire*, a grammar, a magician's catalog of persuasion and manipulation.

Before looking at the historical role of the artist as magician, I would like to briefly examine some possible psychological models behind the need to persuade on the part of one interlocutor, and the need to be persuaded on the part of the other. Consistent with Ball's philosophy, he holds two opposing views: one dark and base, one luminous and exalted. Sadean philosophy represents the former. Sade writes of "normal" society's need to employ persuasion as a means to ensure self-perpetuation. The persuader wields language in the form of ego in order to guarantee his own propagation. If the Sadean goal is to revert to an "abnormal," more natural presocialized existence unmotivated by procreative desire (to revert, that is, to homosexuality), language as we know it, prescribed with moral values, must be abandoned for a lower, more perverse form of communication, that is, sound poetry. To relinquish the ego's language in favor of sound poetry is to paint oneself and all others as abominable monstrosities.

If Sadean theory represents the baser of Ball's views on this subject, then anthroposophy characterizes the latter, purer interpretation. Rudolph Steiner tells a different story than Sade. For him, touch, rather than speech, is the sense that determines our recognition of self-identity, for it does not tell us about the world around us but instead creates a barrier between us and the cosmos. (Unlike jellyfish, whose soft bodies meld with the sea, we live in a world of harmful edges and planes, and so our bodies must be hard.) Touch is the sense that informs our individuation. In an anthroposophical interpretation, the ego sense does not presuppose one's cognition of oneself. In fact, it is that which allows the recognition of the other. When one persuades, one must be acutely aware of the listener's capabilities. Persuasion is a delicate and spiritually motivated activity, for it is something of which only humans are capable. It relies upon dialogue between the vanquished and the vanquisher. From this point of view, the purity of sound poetry is something akin to Ball leading his congregation in prayer, for he knows and embraces them as his flock.

Let us now return to the identification of the artist as magician-enchanter in antiquity. The myth of the artist's ability to fool nature and to better god as a creator is attested to in countless classical tales. Xeuxis was the first artist to be lionized in such a way. He paints Helen as a conglomerate of features taken from five beautiful models, the outcome of which is a woman of unsurpassed magnificence. Daedalus is the first in a venerable lineage of artists who are able to imbue life into art and into statuary. The myths suggest that life's hidden meanings circulate throughout the collective fantasies of humankind but can be unveiled only by means of the incantatory skill of the artist. A thing therefore becomes so true to nature that, infused with the illusion of life, it is born as the simulacrum, the golem. At the Cabaret Voltaire, Ball becomes his own costumed statue come to life. Here the circle closes inasmuch as Ball figures as both the artist-magician and as the simulacrum he devises. That is, taking the apocrypha of the artist of legend just a bit further, he paints a figurative *self*-portrait and then animates his own image. (In Kabala, the vivification of the golem is achieved by the pronunciation of all the letters of the alphabet, spoken over each limb of a clay humanoid, combined with one letter of the tetragrammaton, spoken in a secret manner. According to Gershom Scholem, this can culminate in ecstasy.)

Parallels can also be found in classical thought. Although the hermeneutic of ancient Greek naming remains uncertain, some have argued that according to the epic's definition of identity, the thing named was the full embodiment of that thing. Ball's costumed, rock-solid role refers to this conception of self-identity. For the Greeks, individual psychology in any modern sense neither existed nor could be imagined. There was little place for contemplation of oneself outside one's epithet. Epithet was finality. Ulysses was wily; Hector was brave. These were not descriptions but defining attributes. What Ball represents in the Cabaret Voltaire photograph is a statue of the artist as magician come alive. He enacts the hyperreal simulacrum. But he does not simply dissemble. What Ball stages is an ontological collision. For how can a creator present his own image physically as a simulation, since the very notion of simulation implies the absence of the real thing?

Tenderenda provides many instances of simulacra conflated with realities. Is the seer genuine in his pronouncements, or is he a sham caught out by the mob? Ball prefaces each chapter with an explanatory synopsis that allows us to anticipate the consequences of the subsequent action. The end of the prefaced explanation in the first chapter of *Tenderenda* reads: "What are the consequences to be." Ball lays out a series of signs that become embodiments of their recurrence in the costume so as to deride and dehumanize himself as he parades before the crowd on the way to meet his executioner. The clown figure appeals to cruelty. With his nose made unrecognizable, he loses the ability to locate himself outside the world of animals. The nose provides a sense of good and bad. Humans alone possess its peculiar cartilaginous makeup. Noseless, a person has no access to spiritual hygiene. Without even the snout or beak of a beast, the clown is left with nothing but a brutal and gaping hole, an alternate orifice for the pineal eye.

The orifice in question is that of Georges Bataille's "solar anus": the criminal antipode of the otherwise higher third eye of goodness that, like the spirit in Kabala, can lift up, descend, and ascend higher in its striving for cleavage with warmth, the ineffable, and light. At the moment of his execution, the clown is criminal and the criminal is clown. In the climax of public decapitation, he bodies forth the gnostic darkness of rape, violence, and death in the form of a penis head in the throes of a monstrous ejaculation of spirit that marks his passage to somewhere "higher" (whether good or evil). It is the libertine branch of gnosticism that offered cleansing not through asceticism but through indulgence with the play of destruction and carnal depths making up the process of liberation and opposition to procreation. Classic modernist painting abounds with similar idioms, for example, in the work of Tanguy, Ernst, Miró, Brauner, Masson, Bellmer, and other artists. Bataille writes:

> When my face is flushed with blood, it becomes red and obscene.
> It betrays, at the same time, through morbid reflexes, a bloody erection
>   and a demanding thirst for indecency and criminal debauchery.
> For that reason I am not afraid to affirm that my face is a scandal and
>   that my passions are expressed.
> . . . .
> The terrestrial globe is covered with volcanoes, which serve as its anus.
> Although this globe eats nothing, it often violently ejects the contents
>   of its entrails.
> Those contents shoot out with a racket, and fall back, streaming down.[11]

Here we have the artist as maniac, another of Ball's many personae. With his lips tightly pursed, his features slightly askew, and his predisposition toward toothless grins and downcast eyes, is he not the maniac consumed by guilt?

But the light, the purificatory aspect of Ball's sexual ascent subsists (despite Bataille's insistence upon debauchery). In Kabala, sexual ascent occurs as meditation upon the tetragrammaton. Devekut has been linked with an anonymous epistle describing sexual experience:

> It is well known to the masters of Kabbalah that human thought stems from the intellectual soul, which descends from above. And human thought has the ability to strip itself (of alien things) and to ascend and arrive at the place of its source. Then it unites with the supernal entity, whence it comes and it (the thought) and it (its source) becomes one entity. . . . Our ancient sages stated that when the husband copulates with the wife, and his thought unites with the supernal entities, that very thought draws the supernal light downward, and it (the light) dwells upon that very drop (of semen) upon which he directs his intention and thinks upon . . . [and] that this very drop is permanently linked with the brilliant light . . . as the thought on it (the drop) was linked to the supernal entities, and it draws the brilliant light downward.[12]

Mention of "the wife" notwithstanding, the structure in question is essentially antifeminist. In both the anonymous text and that of Bataille, womanhood plays no active role whatsoever. In Ball's own spiritual quest (with Emmy Hennings cast in the part of neutered priestess and keeper of the flame), there is no reason to think that he possessed anything but the most neurotically fearful feelings toward women. The cornerstone of both texts is male preoccupation with ejaculation. Although the latter hints vaguely at the possibility of a procreative impulse, and the first not at all, the only imperative in either is ultimate self-satisfaction. The issue at hand is therefore masturbatory, the thrust homoerotic. This esotericism relies heavily upon the language of brotherhood and rapture (Rosicrucianism, DADA). Never does it reference the social imperative for reproduction. Mulche-Mulche, in "The Grand Hotel Metaphysics," is no more than a vessel (an anti-Mary) who immaculately conceives and gives birth to the anti-Christ DADA. In the passage cited above, "wife" seems to denote only that which goads ejaculation, not someone with whom to experience sexual soul raising through physical or spiritual participation. "To *him* you shall cleave," says Kabala.[13] Given his spiritual androcentrism, his noted feelings toward Hans Leybold, and the hint of an unconsummated marriage with Emmy Hennings, Ball's homosexual tendencies are apparent.

In Kabalistic theosophical thought (and no doubt as it influenced the central Rosicrucian doctrine of the Chemical Wedding), there exists the state of *duparzufim:* the state of two-sided Adam Kadmon (primordial man) before the discrete creation of Eve.[14] Primeval man, prewoman, inhabited a single body with a dual sexual identity combining attributes of maleness and femaleness, sternness and mercy. Masturbatory homosexuality is the only sex he knows. Eve is not an ex-nihilo creation; she is the corporeal bisexual materialization of Adam's maleness. Masculine and feminine attributes operate in two distinct and separate realms. Their autonomy is such that there need exist no compelling attraction between the two. Only in the act of procreation do they approach each other. In Western esoteric thought, primordial man was just that: man, the male homosexual, the sole being who can successfully embody the tetragrammaton emblazoned on the words *judgment* and *mercy,* later bifurcated into Adam and Eve. Within this scheme, the homosexual figures as a cherub, as an adult innocent. He is Ball's DADA artist who, driven by his neurotic complex, strives for pious androgyny through ascetic Catholicism. Philo writes of cherubim gazing at one another in mutual contemplation of their beauty. He explains that one is god, split so that he may act at once as creator and as ruler. Yet another of Ball's masks.

Homosexuality is alluded to often in *Tenderenda*, especially in the short poem "The Red Heavens." In this "landscape from the upper inferno," Ball conjures as protagonists the "aunties from the seventh sphere," an allusion to the circle of sodomites in Dante's *Inferno*. The "Red Heavens" refer to the Cabaret Voltaire, with its cacophony, animal musicians, sound poetry, cries of murder and woe. Dante punishes his peripatetic damned by means of fire snowing down upon them like an Alpine storm. In Ball we find the same falling red skies and an auntie lifting up out of the snow. *Tenderenda* goes beyond the terms of Dante's quest, for whereas Dante moves freely through Hell, to learn, to bear witness, and to empathize with many of its inhabitants, Ball directly experiences every punishment in the course of his descent.

If sexuality spirals in toward the self, the meditation of devekut and the intention of the pineal eye—in both Bataille and Steiner—spiral outward toward the other in support of the group. Through pineal cosmic ejaculation, as it were, thought is made sacrifice for the sect, the secret society, the brotherhood of healing, the DADA brotherhood. Individual purity becomes a means of mutual succor, an anarchistic and atomistic perfection that affirms the collectivity as it affirms the self. The worshiper (Ball in costume) serves as the channel through which the cosmic influx enters the earthly realm. And if an individual can so transform a community, why not civilization as a whole? The Zohar states that he who cleaves to the ineffable in such a way as to mend the split inherent in the universe may rule the world. The laws that he decrees will be fulfilled. Through DADA, Ball declares his role as seer-lawmaker.

Continual recitation of letters and names as a means to accede to the supernatural is a technique encountered in many cultures. The primary difference between the Hindu or Japanese versions of the practice and that of Kabala is that the former rely upon contemplation of a single point or word in pursuit of an inner peace that screens out all externalia. In the latter, the combinations of letters are complex and ever shifting. They are meant to be elaborated upon in hundreds of ways during meditation, which gives rise to an agitated interior state. The result is a hypersensitized excitement meant to be vocalized and accompanied by head and hand motions. Ball on stage at the Cabaret Voltaire is in such a state of frenzy and exhaustion. The ecstasy in question is that which accompanies the bringing to life of the golem, except that here contemplation and activation of the magic inherent in the "name of god" have shifted over to contemplation and activation of the magic inherent in the divine name DADA. Further parallels may be drawn between Ball and the Kabalist Abulafia, particularly as regards DADA's public ambitions. More than just unveiling a mystical technique, Abulafia strove to embed within his esoteric system a theory of language with social consequences. And in a sense, the biblical and rabbinical ban on pronouncing the tetragrammaton is akin to the cultural and societal ban on, and horror of, the DADA movement itself.

But what, who, and where is DADA? It is only natural to wonder whether there might be a way to fully decode Ball's sound poetry. There must exist some correlation between what provides the link between contemplation and utterance of the word (in this case DADA and the sound poems in general) and the mental and spiritual mechanisms that grant access to higher forms of thought. Was Ball striving for a change in inner consciousness? In his diary he states with hindsight that the word DADA is an anagram of the name of Dionysius the Areopagite. Abulafia's Kabalistic program includes a mandala, which like Ball's play on the name of a divine saint, consists in permutations of the names of god.

The controversy concerning the origin of the word DADA recalls Abulafia's philosophical system that allows for a plurality of mystical pathways, instead of prescribing only one. Multiple truths are always simultaneously at play. In addition to devekut, there is *kavvanah,* a meditative method focusing on the intention with which one practices everyday prayer and performs the commandments. If the name of Dionysius the Areopagite is synonymous with a divine *sefirot,* then, according to the process of kavvanah, when Ball contemplates the word DADA and recites (prays) his sound-poetry liturgy, he is attempting to achieve ascension of thought through language into the realm of the sefirot.[15]

What psychological change does this effect? How can we reconcile the stately pose of the mystical leader and priest with the childish stance of the DADA clown (in this case, the innocent rather than the criminal clown)? The sound poems are meditations on the divine supernal force, but from a psychological standpoint they consist in a form of child speech. Theirs is the natural language of autism, a language prelogical and in direct opposition to realistic thought or conceptual thinking. The linguistic (and visual) return to childishness figures among the principal aims of modernism. Childlike autism marks a withdrawal from reality and an embrace of fantasy in lieu of the frustrations of the real world. It also serves as a metaphor for a state of psychic innocence and purity, that is, thought untainted by concept or irony. Ball envisages the new vocabulary of sound poetry as a tool to gain access to the flow of autistic thought. For ordinary language confronts us with a paradox: the words that explain require explanation themselves. The theme of being at a loss for words to explain words is akin to the psychological notion that one is more than what one portrays. It is frequent in poetry. Osip Mandelstam writes:

I have forgotten the
word I intended to say, and
my thought, unembodied,
returns to the realm of
shadows.[16]

Forgotten is the precognitive autistic river flowing deep beneath the surface of language. The lost word is the word that sounds. Paul Celan writes most eloquently of

tunnels of vision
blown into the fog of speech[17]

and

to hew out
word-shadows, to stack them.[18]

He registers his frustration with the clumsiness of the mechanics by which language and thought produce expression. Like Mandelstam, Celan too is lost in a world of forgetfulness:

A ring, for drawing the bow,
sent after a swarm of words,
it plunges behind the world
with the starlings,

when, like an arrow, you whir towards me,
I know, wherefrom,
I forget, wherefrom.[19]

Poetry is an especially powerful medium in which to explore this psycholinguistic formation. An analytical approach presupposes the existence of an a priori "formed intellect," existing outside the fluvial dialectic of the unformed miasma of autistic language. It is for this reason that no extant manuscripts of Ball's sound poems have ever been found. The poems simply exist. They will admit to no editorial manipulation, to no writerly craft. If the sound poems are Kabalistic contemplations, it would be abhorrent to reveal them in any but their most crystalline perfection, for God loves a thing kept secret, and silence is God's greatest praise.

Ball's sound poems amount to sophisticated inquiries into the domain of concept formation. At the beginning of the century, there were two main trends in the study of this phenomenon within the field of linguistics: the method of definition and the method used to study abstraction. The first, in attending to the naming of already finished products, neglected to examine the process by which particular concepts achieve final form. Since a word is defined by means of other words, a certain redundancy results, inasmuch as a word illuminates only an existing experience that the learner has already undergone. The second method relies on the recognition of common traits within a broad range of examples but neglects the semiotics of words themselves. The same procedure undergirds Ball's efforts in his cabaret-laboratory, forcing the audience to attribute arbitrary meaning to sound, thereby leading them back to a site of raw conceptual formation.

I have mentioned the notion of "inner speech" as it is conceptualized in esoteric mysticism, but its existence in psycholinguistics is also of some importance. Early linguists (post-Saussure) felt that three possible processes formed inner speech: verbal memory (as when reciting something silently by rote); ordinary speech minus sound (hence, a diminished form of normal speech); or the sum total of all that precedes vocalized speech. The opposite of vocalized speech, inner speech is language turned to thought rather than thought manifest as language. It addresses the self (and God) rather than the other.

If the DADA cult of childishness is explained as a form of psychological egocentrism, then inner speech hearkens back to the time of primary autism and the beginnings of socialization. Childish modes of expression in DADA helped the movement to directly break away from the mold of bourgeois morality (which relies heavily on developed and vocalized postegocentric language). Ball used sound to express presocialized thought, much as the surrealists would later employ automatism and other trance games to achieve the same ends. The goal was to bypass ossified "adult" thought and to tap again into a communicative world of past innocence. The complexity of inner speech resides in its elliptical nature. From a linguistic standpoint, the main features that differentiate it from vocalized speech are a peculiar syntax and an inherent incompleteness. Condensations of outward speech, as well as portrayals of inner speech, abound in twentieth-century literature and indicate a striving for greater psychological depth. We find them in Joyce and Woolf, Tolstoy and Stein. Ball's poems are simply a more radical exploration of the same territory. A reduction of language to mere sound presupposes approaching words from a visceral internal standpoint rather than as external conveyors of ideas. Sense consists not in meaning, as conventionally understood, but in the embodiment of a full consciousness (as understood by mysticism). The definition of a word or sound offers little more than a minor facet in understanding its meaning, for it sheds little light on innuendo, connotation, and irony.

Ball's highly original agglutination of words and sounds both in the poems and in *Tenderenda* showcases his effort to overcome the limitations of conventional language use by plumbing a more powerful, egocentric language. His words are made up of phonemes so saturated with sense that they defy definition by means of normal words. His vocabulary becomes an esoteric one, reserved only for initiates. Inner speech and sound poetry operate unencumbered by and independent of ordinary linguistic rules. If in outer speech thought is connected to words, then in the form of speech crystallized by the DADA sound poem, words atrophy and vanish as they become pure expressions of thought beyond language. They are a condition of ideas that cannot possibly be served up on the altar of words. To situate inner speech deep inside language, however, is not to sever it from the realm of action. The sound-poem recitations and other activities at the Cabaret Voltaire fall within the boundaries of what, in the context of modernism, is known as the gratuitous act. That which produces shock in a repulsive or absurd display is the imagination unchained. DADA carried this to the extreme, defiantly opposing Plato's plea for exorcism of the imagination. The gratuitous or anarchistic act—the latter refers here to individual freedom pursued in nonspiritual terms—was often cruel and monstrous. Its DADA emblem is the trickster clown, the preposterous acrobat of an orgiastic creed of gnostic origin laden with Sadean overtones. Transgressive and outrageous, sexually perverse, the wild imaginative act violates conventional corporeal rules. *Tenderenda* is rife with such acts, and no less so Ball's psychic life.

All the inhabitants of "Satanopolis," Chapter V of *Tenderenda*, are monsters of this sort. Consider the following passage:

"That's a very pretty rabbit flusher you've got there," said Mr. Schmidt
    to Mr. Schultz.
"Spinozan affront!" Mr. Meyer said to Mr. Schmidt. Then he mounted
    his nag, which was his weakness, and rode away annoyed.

Homosexual innuendo permeates this exchange between characters whose very names confirm they are the most common of subjects in the underworld city. But the passage hints at more than just homosexuality, which is not entirely transgressive as it perpetuates codes of behavior. It refers specifically to sodomy. For Sade, sodomy is the defining gesture of perversity, since it simulates procreation, flaunting its disregard for natural and societal mores. In the above quote the question is, exactly who gets mounted? In Satanopolis, the perverted make up the entire commonality. When the Devil beseeches Lilienstein to defend himself from charges that he is different from the rest of the lawless and debauched populace of Satanopolis, Lilienstein denies such difference exists and, in a desperate attempt to save himself, begins a scatological apology for his love of laxatives and enema apparatuses. Spinoza is invoked in the "rabbit-flusher" passage because his philosophy hinges upon a duality between God and nature. Nature seeks to recover her most active power, the power to destroy and to transgress, thereby naturalizing deviance and allowing for a world populated by "weak" and aberrant men. This type of realm, feared by Spinoza, becomes a place of infinite possibility for Sade. If the Spinozan God is a state of goodness and plenitude wherein nothing new is ever imaginable, then transgression becomes the precondition for imagination to thrive. In Kabala, the imagination is highly prized as the means by which prophecy can be achieved. Consider the following text: "The philosophers have already written on the issue of prophecy, saying that it is not improbable that there will be a person to whom matters will appear in his imaginative faculty, comparable to that which appears to the imaginative faculty in a dream. All this while someone is awake, and all his senses are obliterated, as the letters of the divine name [are] in front of his eyes. . . . All this while holy letters are in front of his eyes. . . . This is the sleep of prophecy."[20] Trancelike states allow artists to give their imagination free rein so that it may shape a world of prophecy. These varying views of imagination further flesh out Ball's conception of the universal artist. A conception that accounts in part for his uncanny prescience with regard to the events leading up to World War II, the historical advent of the Hitler magus, and the war itself. Take, for instance, the following passage from *Tenderenda* presignifying the crematoria at Auschwitz: "He passes lamp-lit towers, and high blast furnaces where dead . . . corpses burn through the night."[21]

For Ball, imagination was more than a means to prophecy and purity. It was also a tool that unleashed the many facets of the prophet-artist: the monstrous abomination, the maniac, the trickster, the deranged clown playing on his status as victim, the self-lionizing magician who creates a truth more truthful than nature itself. He is the tyrant orator, the trance mystic, the childish buffoon, the compulsive juvenile with the adolescent emotionalism of the painter, the writer, the seer, the demon, the messiah, and the torturer. Ball's artist is the epitome of DADA sensibility. He is the heteroclite deviant composite that manages to exist comfortably within society by fusing the strange and the familiar. His is an evil pastiche, a brutal bricolage. He is Hitler.

This complex figure fueled by the imagination's untamed potential is born out of Ball's great admiration for Sade, who embodies the natural man unencumbered by moral restrictions. Sade represents primary urges unfettered by psychology, capable of the most extraordinary evil, deconstructive negativity, and infantilism. He feels nothing for his actions, his sole aim being to vivify premoralistic impulses. These transgressive drives are sustained through the pursuit of outrage. In Sade, outrage becomes a total experience and an end in itself.

DADA lashed out with Sadean outrage. Outrage aimed at nothing in particular. Outrage for the sake of outrage. Hence, in *Tenderenda*, the constant parade of characters in the guise of thugs, gangs, lowlifes, and mobs attacking, chasing, bringing to trial, or devouring the innocent outsider for no apparent reason other than to revel in mistaken identity. The novel is filled with spaces and landscapes so transgressive that outrage among the inhabitants is the norm. What good is outrage, after all, if it cannot gel into a permanent reality, a lawless underworld such as Satanopolis, the upper inferno of the Red Heavens, the lobby of the Grand Hotel Metaphysics? To the list add the Cabaret Voltaire, as described in the chapter "Laurentius Tenderenda." Here Ball casts himself in the role of Don Quixote espousing the "basic essence of astral cannonale." A new Christ for a new century, he will wield his cross rather than bear it, never knowing if he belongs to the world above or the world below.

Consideration of this expressionist vein in DADA has led some to conclude that the movement declined because of its inability to overcome a reifying concept of art based solely on destruction. The very thing that Walter Benjamin applauds in DADA, its ability to render authentic (by its contesting nature) even the tiniest fragments of daily life, Theodor Adorno condemns as obscurantist violence. His views are amplified by Simone Weil, who decries DADA as licentious and as the moral and artistic equivalent of the sacking of towns.

Such views attend only to the lower half, if you will, of Ball's polar program. In *Tenderenda* there remain defenders of the "up above" who champion a far purer conception of childishness. Goodness appears in the form of Musikon (who is beauty) on the balcony of the Grand Hotel Metaphysics. Goodness appears as the Jubilant Ass, a recurring character related to the hobbyhorse. "They go driving to a gallop their three-seater donkey," reads the text, alluding to a beast who, like the Mercurial Ass of Giordano Bruno, protects clear thinkers from the pedantry of the academicians. This is the colorful ass that Mr. and Mrs. Goldkopf mount in order to descend, in leisurely fashion, into the precipice of the beyond. Here they chase the journalist Lilienstein in the form of a bird; there they chase the brooding hen with her alms bags. Like Lilienstein, Koko the Green God flies freely until caught and caged. In the final chapter,

Mr. and Mrs. Goldkopf inhabit a realm that exists as the book's (relatively) happy ending, as it were, only to witness depravity's encroachment, in the last words of the text, into their world: "In glaring light: the depraved."

Again we return to gnostic antipodes as the passkey to Ball's beliefs and biography. Does not the form of the hobbyhorse itself—the DADA in question—signalize a present in stasis, for it goes nowhere? Yet, once rocked, its seesaw motions encapsulate a dual existence of past and future, with no rest permitted. It must run endlessly in place. It finds peace only when, pushed aside, it is abandoned and ignored. For Ball there is no choosing just one aspect of being. In his DADA life, good and evil necessarily coexist, emblematized by the constant rocking motion of the hobbyhorse.

Ball's vision of evil is always closely linked to the landscape of the underworld. If the original purpose of Hell, with its everlasting torments, was to serve as a deterrent to evil doings among the living, then Ball aligns himself with the early Church Fathers. In *Tenderenda*, Hell ruled by Satan endures for eternity. It is a fully described negative double to Paradise. The artist, like the hobbyhorse, rocks between one realm and the other. Trials and scenes of public outcry figure prominently in the novel, suggesting that life itself is a trial wherein free will and change may be contemplated but never realized. Repentance (for all but the Ball-Machetanz-Lilienstein character) is notably absent in *Tenderenda*. Instead one finds pain as a stand-in for justice. Its infliction causes little discomfort for those who witness it, so long as they believe that good is being served. Executions are and remain public spectacles: the clown as convict led to the gallows. But within Ball's novel of pain, there are occasional glimmers of hope. A "club of visionaries" (the confraternity of DADA-Rosicrucians) surfaces every now and then, unlocking an unexpected passage from Hell to a radiant new age.

So the hobbyhorse rocks. In the chapter "Bulbo's Prayer and the Roasted Poet," it dips in the direction of a breathtakingly horrific apocalypse; in "Mr. and Mrs. Goldkopf," it tips back toward a positive apocalypticism. Never in *Tenderenda* is the symbolic language subtle. It is always dense, elliptical, and extreme, for its source is Ball's memories of the wild revelry at the Cabaret Voltaire and of his night as the "Knight of Glossy Paper." The entire novel is a reminiscent reworking of this event. There are repeated abstract descriptions of modern dancers in costumed skits that recall the Von Laban dances of Sophie Taeuber, Mary Wigman, and other entertainers who performed at the cabaret. Ball writes: "We are dancing beasts in towering headgear. We grapple with sobriety. Fruitlessly so."[22] Through a haze of drunkenness, Ball sees the unrestrained movements employed in modern dance as a pure artistic expression.

To understand the apocalyptic strain in Ball's writing, it is necessary to look both at apocalyptic literature itself and at the historical milieu within which it flourished. Apocalyptic literature arose in the midst of an era characterized by syncretism (like that of the turn of the twentieth century): the period of intertestamental Hellenism, roughly from 200 B.C. to A.D. 100. Any reader of *Tenderenda* will find familiar Ball's allusions to "a stream of Chaldean wisdom and Chaldean sages, astrologers, popular philosophers, itinerant preachers, miracle workers and charlatans which in Hellenistic times spread over the world."[23] Does this not also describe the many faces of the twentieth-century artist? "Hymn 3" in *Tenderenda*, after all, begins with the invocation of the Chaldean archangel. And let us remember Donnerkopf in his tower in the first chapter, "The Rise of the Seer," setting the stage for the rest of the novel.

Ball felt a deep personal affinity to apocalyptic literature, in particular to the Book of Daniel, the first and greatest of all such texts. He writes that he "take[s] the whole story [of Daniel] as if it had been arranged for [him]. As if it had been planned to play into [his] hands."[24] At the time of writing this, it must have seemed to him that the end was close at hand. He refers to Switzerland as a "birdcage surrounded by roaring lions," the lions of war and of cultural-moral dissolution.[25] *Tenderenda* is meant both as a mirror of the times and as a DADA vehicle, a text that at once bears witness and works to shape the times. In sounding its own war cry, like Hellenistic apocalyptic literature, it acts as propaganda, instructing a new breed of artist-zealots to do battle on both physical and spiritual grounds.

Certain of the standard themes in Judeo-Christian apocalyptics can be readily identified in *Tenderenda*. There is the interplay of two ages: in the first chapter we find the sorrow of the final days when the Messiah (the twentieth-century artist) is rejected and the world is cut down; and in the last chapter we read of hope in the coming of the messianic age as Koko the Green God resides in the alphabet tree of life. Also represented are the judgment of the world, the resurrection of the dead, and the future lot of the wicked and the righteous. In short, Ball writes in a conventional apocalyptic genre. Like Daniel in exile with his three companions, Ball and his companions must remain true to their religion—in this case art—in the face of temptation. He is granted the gift of prophesying the future not of his own exilic present but of the subsequent history of his homeland and the rise of Hitler.

In his writing Ball places contemporary events under a dense cloak of biblical allegory. Like the early Jewish syncretic writers, he relies on a promiscuous admixture of sources ranging from native to foreign to mythological to esoteric to just plain quirky and uncanny. "Bulbo's Prayer and the Roasted Poet" offers a commentary on World War I and the German crisis in a language that melds apocalyptic elements with those borrowed from the greatest of the Old Testament's prophetic books, Ezekiel: a language of fantastic imagery whose symbolism is wide-ranging and whose protagonist is a more powerful and transcendent god. The account of the battle between God and Gog (the threat from the north—Germany—who, when destroyed, will usher in a messianic world) seems to have shaped God's dance with death in *Tenderenda*. Ancient prophetic writing was engaged writing. It directly addressed the present state of the prophet's homeland. This helps to explain how Ball imagined himself as a preacher who both revels in and abhors his people's sins in the name of God. He wields the lawlessness of the artist as a weapon against the lawlessness of the state.

As already hinted, *Tenderenda* is concerned not just with the vicissitudes of war, men, and nations but also with the great eschatological themes: men and angels, Heaven and Hell, the beginning and the end, the struggle between the kingdom of God and the kingdom of Satan. The book is a compilation of esoteric sources secretly handed down from the birth of time. It is the oracle, the seer, the grimoire of a sect made up of DADA artists and their brethren. Like the sacred texts of the Essenes, a monastic brotherhood of Jews, the contents of which they swore never to divulge, *Tenderenda* will also continue to be passed from one generation to the next in a tradition of mystery, power, initiation, and contemplation of the ineffable. *Tenderenda* is a book of revelations. Or so Ball intended.

Of course, with Ball there is always a twist. Unlike the antediluvian Noah or Enoch, who were privy to esoteric knowledge because of their inborn wisdom and their subsequent initiation, Ball's characters are less than biblically wise. They are artists whose wisdom is reducible to an act of raw witnessing, registered by a sensory mass of flesh and a neurotic psyche. As with Ball's surrogate Daniel, this fleshly wisdom is flawed. It cannot be tapped or interpreted without the aid of divine wisdom, for human skill alone will not suffice. But the DADA Seer can at least report. In the cabaret setting he can speak divine words to the people. In *Tenderenda* he can write what he observes.

But why the truncated, violently elliptical nonlinear prose? If scenes from the Cabaret Voltaire and World War I are judged inexpressible, then a sober common tongue simply will not suffice. An exotic new language must be devised, one that openly embraces poetry, myth, and arcane symbolism. As already noted, Ball relies upon gnostic intertestamental models to define character motivation and place in *Tenderenda*. Images, characters, and incidents recur from one chapter to another but constantly shift so that their successive appearances often seem disjointed or clouded. In one chapter we may find a complex tableau that later returns in such a fragmentary form that the two seem unrelated in meaning. Scale changes indiscriminately. Strange details and metaphors with no bearing on the outcome of events riddle the narrative, providing a multifaceted, kaleidoscopic vision of some larger truth. This continues through the very end of the text where, cast as Enoch, Ball conjures himself as Metatron, prince of the divine presence comprising the many Kabalistic names he has meditated upon as DADA, and shakes the godless from the world.

Tenderenda drinks long and deeply from the font of biblical and intertestamental writing; so much so that a full account of its borrowings would require a far lengthier analysis than the present one. Confirming signs abound. "Bulbo's Prayer and the Roasted Poet" alone alludes to the anti-Christ, Satan, the Babylonian mythical origins of the Leviathan providing the messianic banquet for the remaining revenants, and much more.

Ball's tumultuous existence had been devoted to casting himself in every role within this fantastic genre. Through conversion, he hoped to free himself from this painful pathology. So it is perhaps no great surprise that, by the summer of 1920, when he completed *Tenderenda*, Ball had long since distanced himself from the movement whose history it chronicled. His diary, *Flight Out of Time*, eloquently bears witness to just what a tortuous inner trial the writing of *Tenderenda* had been for him. With its conclusion he hoped to finally lay to rest the darkness and to bury the demons that had long tormented him:

> Today I finished my *Phantastischer Roman*. . . . I can compare the little book only with that soundly constructed magic chest the old Jews thought Asmodeus was locked in. In all those seven years I have kept on playing with these words and sentences in the midst of torments and doubts. Now the book is finished, and it is a real liberation. I hope that all those fits of malice are buried in it, of which Saint Ambrose says:
>
> Procul recedant somnia
> Et noctium phantasmata,
> Hostemque nostrum comprime.
>
> From dreams,
> from nighttime fantasies,
> shield our eyes,
> tread upon our foe.[26]

NOTES

I have chosen to keep the word DADA in caps throughout my essay regardless of whether I am referring to the historical movement specifically or to the concepts the word has come to represent in general. My reasoning is consistent with the thesis that the letters D-A-D-A form an anagrammatical equivalent with the letters of the tetragrammaton Yod-Hey-Vov-Hey. After all, whether noun or adjective, the ineffable can never be less than the ineffable.

1 On *devekut*, see Gershom Scholem, *Kabbalah* (New York: New American Library, 1978), 174–76.

2 Ball, *Flight Out of Time*, 169.

3 Cited from Frances A. Yates, *The Rosicrucian Enlightenment* (Boulder: Shambala , 1978), 242.

4 Ibid., 243.

5 From Huelsenbeck's "Dada Lives," cited in Ball, *Flight Out of Time*, 246.

6 Ball, "First Dada Manifesto," in *Flight Out of Time*, 220.

7 Ibid., 66.

8 Porphyry, *Ad Marcellam*, cited in Hans Jonas, *The Gnostic Religion*, 2d rev. ed. (Boston: Beacon Press, 1963), 61.

9 *Pistis Sophia*, cited in Jonas, *The Gnostic Religion*, 65.

10 Gnostic fragment cited in ibid., 72.

11 Georges Bataille, "The Solar Anus," in *Visions of Excess: Selected Writings 1927–1939*, ed. Alan Stoekl, trans. Alan Stoekl et al., Theory and History of Literature 14 (Minneapolis: University of Minnesota Press, 1991), 8.

12 Moshe Idel, *Kabbalah: New Perspectives* (New Haven: Yale University Press, 1988), 52.

13 The phrase is frequent in Kabala and is of biblical derivation: "And unto Him shall you cleave" (Deuteronomy 13:5).

14 On the Chemical Wedding in Rosicrucianism, see Yates, *The Rosicrucian Enlightenment*, 59–69. On *du-parzufim* and the concept of the primordial Adam engendered by the raising and lowering of the cosmic balance, see Scholem, *Kabbalah*, 130–44.

15 In Kabala, *Sefirot* refers to the realm of divine emanations and attributes, inaccessible to human perception, within which God's creative power manifests itself.

16 Osip Mandelstam, "The Swallow," cited in Lev Vygotsky, *Thought and Language*, trans. Alex Kozulin (Cambridge: M.I.T. Press, 1986), 210.

17 Paul Celan, "Under the Flood," in *Last Poems*, trans. Katharine Washburn and Margret Guillemin (San Francisco: North Point Press, 1986), 95.

18 "Snow-Voice," ibid., 111.

19 "A Ring, for Drawing from the Bow," ibid., 183.

20 Idel, *Kabbalah*, 105.

21 Ball, *Tenderenda*, 48.

22 Ibid., 101.

23 D. S. Russell, *The Method and Message of Jewish Apocalyptic* (Philadelphia: Westminster Press, 1964), 18.

24 Ball, *Flight Out of Time*, 34.

25 Ibid., 34.

26 Ibid., 186–87. Translated from the Latin by J. Schnapp.